LEADERSHIP POINTS OF CONNECTION

Expanding Your Impact through Meaningful Connections

Dr. Bobbi Y. Cumpston

ISBN 979-8-89130-641-7 (paperback)
ISBN 979-8-89243-978-7 (hardcover)
ISBN 979-8-89130-642-4 (digital)

Christian Faith Publishing
832 Park Avenue
Meadville, PA 16335
www.christianfaithpublishing.com

Printed in the United States of America

CONTENTS

INTRODUCTION

If your actions inspire others to dream more, learn more,
do more, and become more, you are a leader.

—John Quincy Adams

What is a "point of connection"? A connection is a relationship in which a person, thing, or idea is linked or associated with something else. Points of connection are specific interactions with others that bring about illumination, creative innovation, or impactful discussion, adding value to the individual or the relationship. Personal relationships with family and friends, businesses, volunteer organizations, churches, and places we live and work are areas we can influence to improve the community. Points of connection are with people we lead, guide, or mentor that add value to their lives. Global points of connection help expand our worldview, educate us about other cultures, and challenge assumptions and biases. With points of connection, we can help edify and uplift others, share education, and help those less fortunate or in need.

A point of connection can also unite people together for a common purpose or goal. A point of connection can be a moment that changes a situation, enlightens a mind, or develops a beneficial solution to a problem. An individual can experience many points of connection over time. Some connections, like family or friends, last a lifetime. It is where you can provide, nurture, educate, protect, love, and help them find their purpose. Other points of connection are brief or seemingly insignificant and yet can change your course of action.

Leadership is a point of connection. When you lead, there must be followers. Who you are as a leader matters. Your personal leadership statement helps define your mission, meaning, values, and reasons for why you do what you do.[1] A strong sense of purpose, resiliency, servant-leadership qualities, authenticity, and transformation helps build your leadership character so you can prepare for points of connection with followers. Leaders build hardiness and preparation, make decisions, are involved and committed, and challenge others to develop skills, talents, and leadership qualities.[2] Moreover, you determine your internal leadership qualities by defining your code of conduct that upholds your personal and professional reputation.

Meaningful connections include people, power, position, purpose, peace, and person. Each connection represents a relationship with someone who added value to your life through an idea or discussion that illuminated, encouraged, or brought peace about a decision or situation. The people we engage with through family, work, or community should bring peace and help us discover our purpose. Meaningful connections can be intentional meetings or spontaneous moments we remember because of what transpired.

When you lead others or encounter them through a point of connection, look for the best in them. Help them find and uplift their strengths, encouraging them to pursue their work actively. The result may be self-development or professional development, but it is often the intentional search for significance. It is through discovering who we are, what we have, and how to walk in it that we find the keys to freedom, joy, well-being, and welfare. Points of connection, operating in love for one another, can guide you in discovering your purpose and passion that put your life into perspective.

---

[1] Sosik and Jung 2018.
[2] Citrin and Weiss 2016.

Position
Power
PEOPLE

People of Connection

We form relationships throughout our lives in every capacity, from family to friends, coworkers, and acquaintances. Some relationships last a lifetime, and some are brief encounters. Whether good or bad, impactful relationships create memories, cause actions, and produce emotional responses that shape our connections to others. People of connection refer to those we relate to in some capacity. Relationships happen daily, and when we are intentional about our interactions, we can positively impact each other.

Connections with people happen in multiple areas, from family to business, community, and across the globe. Relationship types can help you determine the connecting purpose and how to develop it with intention. Meaningful family and friend relationships develop over a lifetime. Relationships with friends and family should give each person a foundation of love, honor, and value. Thriving family and friend relationships should encourage and know each other to build and maintain good connections. C. S. Lewis said, "Friendship is born at that moment when one man says to another: 'What! You too? I thought that no one but myself.'" People come and go, but those with whom you connect for life share a deep and abiding friendship.

People of connection can be workplace, community, or government leaders. Leaders have the opportunity to develop connections with followers and peers who can benefit from you and you from them. Leaders make connections and network and develop mutually beneficial relationships. Some say leaders are born, and others say that leaders are made. Northouse defines leadership as "a process whereby an individual influences a group of individuals to achieve a common goal."[3] Leaders are people of connection who educate, guide, influence, and mentor followers.

Leaders as people of connection can be viewed by their traits or leadership process. Traits are internal qualities or talents that support the thought that there are natural-born leaders.[4] However, leadership as a process is external, meaning that behaviors are observed and learned, opening leadership to everyone.[5] Leadership includes multiple traits and strategies that underscore the necessity of connections surpassing a simple leader-follower relationship.[6] Several leadership theories help define people of connection and how each contributes to positive relations.

Authentic leadership

Authentic leaders have four distinct components: self-awareness, internalized moral perspective, balanced processing, and relational transparency.[7] Self-awareness is a process of understanding who you are, your strengths and weaknesses, core values and beliefs, motivations, and emotions.[8] Self-awareness also includes understanding your impact on others. An internalized moral perspective guides the decisions and actions of the authentic leader. Moreover, ethical standards and values drive the decisions and behaviors of a leader rather than allowing group or societal pressure to control them.[9]

The authentic leader is intentional about relationships with followers through balanced processing. Balanced processing objectively

---

[3] Northouse 2019.
[4] Ibid.
[5] Ibid.
[6] Winston and Patterson 2006.
[7] Avolio, Walumbwa, and Weber 2009.
[8] Northouse 2019.
[9] Ibid.

considers others' viewpoints or perspectives before making decisions.[10] Authentic leaders cultivate trust, place others' needs before their own, and help followers align their interests to create a common good.[11] Leaders are at their best when leading from the heart, with character and integrity that ensure followers of their honesty in relationships and work, showing relational transparency.[12] Authentic leaders inspire followers to genuine actions that fulfill an organization's vision.[13] When authentic leaders become people of connection, their authenticity shines through their words and actions to motivate and encourage others.

Authentic leaders provide an atmosphere that encourages creativity and innovation through sincerity, openness, and transparency.[14] Moreover, authenticity is a positive means of developing followers with the expected effects of inclusiveness, empathy, and ethical decisions.[15] Leader behaviors are essential in encouraging a creative environment that produces positive, measurable results. Changes and uncertainty create a desire for trustworthy leaders who are honest and good leaders.[16] The essence of an authentic leader is purposeful, value centered, relational, self-disciplined, and compassionate.[17] Implementation of authentic leadership builds reciprocal relationships with purpose and integrity.

People of connection who are authentic leaders empower individuals to act as they see fit, with the freedom to choose their actions through autonomy and personal choice. However, authentic leaders also question the morality and ethics of plans and decisions. Societies value autonomy and self-determination. However, authentic leadership examines the underlying decisions and choices that compromise values and integrity. People of connection provide balance and

---

[10] Ibid.

[11] Ibid.

[12] Kouzes and Posner 2017, Northouse 2019.

[13] Winston and Patterson 2006.

[14] Cerne, Jaklic, and Skerlavaj 2013.

[15] Gardner et al. 2005.

[16] Northouse 2019.

[17] George 2003.

perspective, focusing on abilities and motivation outside selfishness, leading to positive interactions and results.

Authentic leaders with high levels of emotional intelligence perceive, appraise, and express others' emotions.[18] Emotional intelligence is a connection that helps leaders discern emotions, identify problems, and help followers engage in creative, productive solutions, often with collaboration and interaction with coworkers.[19] Personal histories and trigger events are relatable experiences that build trust between leaders and followers and create positive relationships, resulting in personal growth and development.[20] Authentic people of connection network with others to encourage excellence in personal and professional development. Performance, efficiency, and effectiveness combine to equal excellence.[21] People of connection who combine authenticity and excellence model achievement, demonstrating leadership qualities that can inspire others.

Transformational leadership

When people of connection model authenticity and lead others, they can bring out a transformation in followers. Transformational leadership is a process where people connect and engage with others, creating a connection and raising motivation and morality.[22] Transformational leaders are inclined to challenge and develop individuals into quality leaders through vision, innovation, coaching, and mentoring.[23] Transformational leaders actively participate in the development and growth of followers, which, in turn, benefits the organization's mission.

Transformational leaders discuss the importance of values, beliefs, and purpose with followers. Individual values and beliefs shape the personal and professional search for purpose and meaning.

---

[18] Zhou and George 2003.

[19] Ibid.

[20] Gardner et al. 2005.

[21] Engstrom 1976.

[22] Northouse 2019.

[23] Sosik and Jung 2018.

Connecting with others through similar values and beliefs encourages choices and actions aligned with those values and beliefs. Moreover, when people of connection set aside self-interest for the good of the group, learning and innovation become positive outcomes.[24] Such results deepen transformational connections by broadening perspectives and motivating creativity, contributing to collective ideas, goals, and decisions benefitting the organization.[25] The organization's joint mission and future strategies depend on the transformational leader to connect people with creative ideas and innovation that achieve the ideal performance and challenge the status quo.[26]

Transformational leaders also act as coaches or mentors. A coach is "someone trained and devoted to guiding others into increased competence, commitment, and confidence."[27] A mentor imparts knowledge and experience to guide, provide wisdom, and counsel, whereas a coach encourages someone to draw on their own experiences, thoughts, and decisions toward growth and change. Coaches and mentors can be valuable connections who challenge ideas, increase knowledge, and push individuals toward achieving goals. Organizational coaching has also increased commitment and job satisfaction and improved teamwork and communication.[28] In addition, coaching has the potential for a ripple effect, meaning that the quality of interactions with others improves psychological well-being.[29] As mentors or coaches, people of connection provide valuable relationships for growth, challenges, and leadership development.

Mentoring is also a great way of encouraging opportunities for growth in an organization. A mentorship culture is about coaching others, assessing their performance, and providing feedback to mentees.[30] Mentoring can also offer a cultural change to the organization that expands the leader's view from technical and political aspects to

---

[24] García-Morales, Jiménez-Barrionuevo, and Gutiérrez-Gutiérrez 2012.
[25] Ibid.
[26] Sosik and Jung 2018.
[27] Hudson 1999.
[28] Boysen, Charry, Amerie, and Takagawa 2018.
[29] O'Connor and Cavanaugh 2006.
[30] Kouzes and Posner 2017.

people. Cultural change assesses a problem, how the existing culture contributes to the problem, and designs ways to evolve the culture toward a positive solution.[31] Innovative solutions, cultural change, and growth depend greatly on leadership to connect with employees and improve an organization.

Servant leadership

Servant leaders are especially significant people of connection. "Servant leaders put followers first, empower them, and help them develop their full personal capacities." [32] The hallmarks of servant leadership ensure those served are healthy, wise, free, autonomous, and gain benefit from service.[33] Servant leadership is virtuous, exemplifying excellence by focusing on followers through behaviors and attitudes.[34]

Servant leadership is a relationship between leaders and followers rooted in love, focused on the individual rather than the organization.[35] Servant leaders meet organizational goals and objectives by empowering individuals.[36] Biblical leaders demonstrate leadership by responding to a call to action with a flexible personal approach that meets the community's needs.[37] Servant leadership is a spiritual calling that proceeds from inside the leader and manifests outside.[38] Servant leadership foundations applied internally result in growth as a leader serving others. Serving others is a high call, applicable to any organization.

Biblical leadership principles transcend culture and time and apply to leadership challenges experienced in all areas of life.[39]

---

[31] Schein and Schein 2016.
[32] Northouse 2019.
[33] Greenleaf 1977.
[34] Patterson 2003.
[35] Ibid.
[36] Ghosh, Koustab, and Naresh 2017.
[37] Agosto 2005.
[38] Crowther 2018.
[39] Bell 2014.

Servant-leadership principles and traits place individuals and relationships ahead of the organization or community but do not exclude the organization's goals. Aligning individual and organizational goals and objectives creates a mutually beneficial and dynamic relationship. Paul's example of servant leadership applied to every community and culture he encountered. Biblical servant-leader principles transcend time to present-day leaders, organizations, and communities. When servant leaders empower individuals, they can add significance to the organization with internal values, principles, and relationships. Organizational culture and context also influence servant leadership in applying external manifestations.[40] Actions appropriate to the organization or industry are essential considerations in servant leadership.

When actioning the principles of servant leadership, the outcomes include personal growth and performance, organizational performance, and societal impact.[41] The results of servant leadership empower followers and maximize their potential. In turn, empowered followers contribute to enhanced organizational performance, positively impacting society. Servant-leadership principles are, in a sense, perpetual because they do not stop with the individual. The results affect many areas of society and culture.

With a selfless mindset, servant leaders, as people of connection, carry influence in any area and industry. The servant leader focuses on the individual and leads them in growth and development, positively impacting the organization.[42] Servant leaders operate from knowing who they are; their purpose is to serve and lead. Servant leadership is a calling that proceeds from the inside out.[43] Service comes from the heart, from a position of love to the outside, demonstrated through service. The servant leader connects with others from love with a desire to uplift, provoke, and propel followers to their best selves. In Mark 10:43 (TPT), Jesus says, "You are to lead by a different model. If you want to be the greatest one, live as one called

---

[40] Northouse 2019.
[41] Ibid.
[42] Coetzer, Bussin, and Geldenhuys 2017.
[43] Bell and Habel 2010.

to serve others." Jesus's example was of servant leadership rather than the example of leaders who ruled by oppression.

Servant leaders apply listening and compassion skills to build trusting relationships or connections with followers to empower them.[44] Empowerment requires continuous growth and development by encouraging and activating individual talent.[45] Servant leaders also help followers develop a vision and align thinking and outcomes that help fulfill the vision.[46] Servant leadership combines humility and behaviors that encourage action and efficacy.[47] Humility shows a willingness to place others ahead of self, giving support and credit to uplift and inspire.[48]

From a biblical perspective, servant leadership proceeds from the inside out, from a position of knowing who you are in Christ and serving from that position. Jesus lived from the inside out, knowing who His Father was and operating in His mission and calling. In John 8:28, Jesus says He does nothing on His initiative but only what He sees the Father doing. Servant leadership must be practiced through relationships, just as Jesus had a relationship with the Father. Servant leaders model the way by defining, affirming, and aligning actions with shared values.[49]

Servant leaders are revolutionary. Servant leadership is paradoxical in that they serve first and then lead. Servant leaders work for the good of an individual's growth and development. Secondary goals are for the good of the organization and the community. As revolutionaries, servant leaders can affect change in organizational culture and society. A servant-leader culture can be high performance with the right people and connections whose values align with the servant-leader culture.[50]

---

44 Coetzer, Bussin, and Geldenhuys 2017.
45 Ibid.
46 Bell and Habel 2010.
47 Sousa and Van Dierendonck 2017.
48 Ibid.
49 Kouzes and Posner 2017.
50 Crowther 2018.

In addition, senior leaders in an organization can affect the culture through consistently upholding and actioning servant-leadership values. The three stages of servant leadership start with preparation, internal character development, and a proper worldview in love.[51] The second stage involves leading from a calling and a purpose. The third stage is creating a legacy of leadership. A leader builds on each level, serving and leading from an internal calling rather than a position.[52] As leaders become confident in their values and know their calling and purpose, they empower followers to grow and develop, leading to a servant-leadership culture, thereby forming a legacy of servant leadership.

Paul's letters are examples of servant leadership in the New Testament that show his priorities were sharing the gospel, building relationships with his followers, and building a community of believers. In Philippians 2:3–4, Paul encourages the Philippians to regard others as more important than self and to look out for personal interests and the interests of others. Humility and selflessness are two qualities Paul emphasizes, which also align with servant leadership.

Internal values

People of connection are self-aware and know who they are, their values, and their moral foundation. They understand what that relationship with others means. When you are self-aware, self-confident, and have self-esteem and self-control, you can positively connect with others. Whether encouraging creativity and innovation or guiding through difficulty, your intentional connections with others help edify and build them up with deliberate care and authenticity.

One of the challenges a leader faces is to define and comprehend the personal, deeply held values that provide guidance and drive. Values include ethics, morals, beliefs, and ideals authentically representing who you are.[53] People of connection can help define

---

[51] Ibid.
[52] Sun 2013.
[53] Kouzes and Posner 2017.

or redefine values and encourage self-evaluation that promotes personal and professional growth. When you define personal values, you desire to have people of connection whose values align with yours.

The values alignment also pertains to organizations. When an employee's values align with the organizational values, their suitability and commitment to the organization increase, as does their desire to remain a long-term employee.[54] Values are an aspect of an organization's culture that becomes cultural DNA taken for granted and shared with new members.[55] The more closely aligned individual and organizational values are, the stronger the corporate culture.[56] People of connection within an organization can help clarify the organizational values, encourage behaviors that match, and help develop solutions when they do not.

Creativity and innovation

People of connection can help redefine values and mission as organizations change and grow through creativity and innovation. As organizations become more dynamic and global, tasks, values, and priorities become more complex, requiring individuals to be perpetual learners.[57] Networking and social skills, knowledge, and personal engagement are competencies that global leaders have and use in solid performances with noticeable results.[58] As people of connection, global leaders are mindful of daily learning through experience and reflection with others.[59] Personal relationships with others provide shared knowledge and experience that enhance personal and professional development, benefitting the individual and the organization.

Connections and networking are essential in a new organization. In addition, cultural assessment, communication, and growth opportunities are also areas worth examining that can contribute to

---

[54] Krajcsák 2018.
[55] Schein 2017.
[56] Krajcsák 2018.
[57] Schein 2017.
[58] Forsyth and Maranga 2015.
[59] Cseh, Davis, and Khilji 2012.

an overview of the organization where leaders can assess areas for positive change. In addition, the vision and mission statements of the organization provide employees with the organizational foundation and purpose. Communication with peers and colleagues helps interactions, provides clarification, opens doors to networking, develops empathy, brings open-mindedness, and challenges assumptions.

Leaders identify problems, drive innovation, and work with others to design positive solutions to impact an organization.[60] Leaders can also take a *renovation* approach, where leaders examine each *room* of the organization for attributes and problems, which will help identify areas for improvement or change.[61] Leaders who model collaboration, knowledge, idea sharing, and information exchange contribute to creativity and innovation in problem-solving.[62] Also known as the leader-member exchange theory, relationships between leaders and followers are esteemed, and the goals of the leader, follower, and organization are advanced.[63]

Global connection

Many organizations operate worldwide, in countries with different laws and cultures than the home office. A global mindset and curiosity help grow your connections to others through opportunities to interact with individuals different from you. Global leaders place into action informal learning during daily work and life experiences and value learning from mistakes.[64] Global leaders also forage for new knowledge and insights about cultures and events worldwide and place themselves in situations that form new relationships. Global connections also need trust to flourish. People of connection use trust and value to transcend cultural barriers and gain insight and understanding on working with others despite their differences.

---

[60] Kouzes and Posner 2017.
[61] Mihalko 2006.
[62] Carmeli, Gelbard, and Reiter-Palmon 2013.
[63] Northouse 2019.
[64] Cseh et al.

Global leaders are visionaries who cross social, cultural, and political boundaries to discover ways to build, cultivate, and connect contributors despite differences.[65] Global leaders continuously learn and grow through knowledge and practice of leadership characteristics.[66] In addition to education, global leaders connect with others who are different to enhance relationships, gain insight, and influence others for growth and connection.[67]

Global leaders with Christian values and beliefs focus on transforming people rather than accumulating material things.[68] It is this mindset and the importance of people that global leaders use to cross barriers between countries, cultures, and prejudices that deter transformation. Scripture supports global leadership through Jesus's mandate to proclaim the gospel to all of creation (Mark 16:15). In Galatians 3:8, Paul tells the Galatian believers that through Abraham, the Gentiles are justified by faith.

Paul's example of global leadership is evident in his training and instruction through his letters to the seven churches. He was aware of cultural, political, and social differences in each city and addressed the followers in those cities with intellectual and social competence. His focus remained on people with the desire to see them grow in their relationship with God and each other. Today's global leaders, especially global Christian leaders, can now effectively integrate Christian and biblical-centric perspectives in leadership that changes the world. Time and context are also important considerations for global leaders, as is the willingness to learn and grow through experiences and knowledge sharing.[69] The global environment is constantly changing, requiring competent global leaders who are intellectually, culturally, and socially mindful. Global leaders are people of connection.

---

[65] Cabrera and Unruh 2012.

[66] Ibid.

[67] Ibid.

[68] Valk 2010.

[69] Stavridis 2017.

Personal and professional development

Leaders also challenge and develop colleagues to progress in professional development, and the organization retains the best and brightest.[70] As a new leader, assessing individuals, the organizational culture, and communication needs provides vital information and assistance in identifying problems and designing solutions. Knowledge sharing, internal and external collaboration, and cultivating positive and creative solutions enhance colleague relationships.[71] Every effort to improve the organization reinforces the collaborative efforts that support the vision and mission statements.

People of connection can awaken creativity and innovation in the workplace, community, or personal lives. Novel and creative ideas or solutions are necessary to improve the human condition.[72] People remain in the status quo or their comfort zone without creativity and innovation. Creativity and innovation involve risk, which is seldom supported by others.[73] However, people of connection can provide the motivation and encouragement that awaken creativity.[74] Organizational people of connection can also provide a positive workplace climate that encourages innovation and creative development.[75] People need growth and development that stretch and challenge them to be and do better than yesterday.

People of connection can share thoughts and ideas that can become bigger and better. Collaboration expands relationships and enhances critical thinking and strategy. As a supply sergeant in the US Army, I was part of a network of soldiers. We networked, shared information and best practices, and built a camaraderie that helped each other. Trying to do the work alone is daunting. Developing relationships and networking with others gave us an unspoken bond that let us know we were not alone and could call on each other in time of need.

---

[70] Sosik and Dongil 2018.
[71] Carmeli, Gelbard, and Reiter-Palmon 2013.
[72] Zhou and George 2003.
[73] Berkun 2010.
[74] Zhou and George 2003.
[75] Ghosh 2014.

One friend served with me on deployment to Kuwait. She and I connected because of our age, deployment experience, and life experiences. We walked through the dust and heat in Camp Buehring, Kuwait, week after week, building such a lasting friendship that we became like sisters. After we returned from Kuwait, I worked away from home for another year, with weekly or monthly commutes.

People of connection also challenge you to be better and to pursue excellence. They challenge your assumptions or thoughts on subjects. I recently connected with a retired professor who taught East Asian history. We had an in-depth discussion about leadership and my doctoral project. He asked challenging questions about leadership, its meaning, and its application. We had a lively and lengthy conversation that encouraged me to be ready to answer questions with critical thought and intention. That is the point of people of connection. They can open doors, challenge assumptions, and introduce you to new possibilities.

We can look to Jesus and the people He encountered for inspiration as people of connection. Jesus connected with people on their level. He inspired followers and chose His disciples who willingly gave up everything to follow Him. You may only meet someone once; when that connection is significant, it leaves a lasting impression and impacts one or both of you no matter how brief the relationship is.

Connection in action

My daughter, Samantha, is a people-of-connection example. Samantha owns a photography business and is an event manager at a local ice hockey rink. She has people of connection who have poured into her photography business through community connections, sound business advice, and hiring her for ongoing photo shoots and social media. Her people of connection mentor her and influence her to stretch and grow, sometimes with discomfort and frustration but always in love. Moreover, that is what people of connection do. They see the potential for greatness in you and work with you to bring it out. They help you connect with a better version of yourself, just as mentors do.

Samantha's employer at the hockey rink saw in her the capabilities for increased responsibility and promotion to a salaried position. Her work ethic and dedication to excellence demonstrated her abilities to those in positions of leadership and authority. With her new job, Samantha networks with business leaders and officials throughout the region to promote her organization and display her leadership qualities to others.

Samantha is now a people of connection. A friend opened a beauty-and-nail salon, and Samantha encourages and influences a young woman like herself. She shares business strategies and encourages her to continue working hard and providing excellent customer service. Samantha also donates her time and photography skills to help promote the salon. The essence of servant leadership is humility with respect for others.[76] People of connection demonstrate servant-leadership qualities when they focus on and care for others.

Brené Brown says,

> I define connection as the energy that exists between people when they feel seen, heard, and valued; when they can give and receive without judgment; and when they derive sustenance and strength from the relationship.[77]

Relationships create a ripple effect, like throwing a stone into a pond. As ripples in the pond expand, so do the relationships and impact that people of connection have on the spaces and people around them. People of connection can multiply this effect by joining with others to influence and impact the world around them. Intentional relationships that form with people of connection are lasting and go beyond superficial pleasantries. Relationships with people of connection are like a garden. It takes time, sowing, and cultivation for your garden to grow and flourish.

---

[76] Bell and Habel 2010.

[77] Brené Brown 2022.

Cultivating relationships is not effortless. Sometimes, you will need to weed out those that are unnecessary. When you value others, you look out for their interests and your own, not in a self-serving or selfish way. Philippians 2:3–4 (NASB) says,

> Do nothing from selfishness or empty conceit, but with humility of mind regard one another as more important than yourselves; do not merely look out for your own interests but also for the interests of others.

Paul was a people of connection who mentored people like Timothy and created a ripple effect that started with his teaching and writing to the new Christian churches in the New Testament. The ripple effect increased and multiplied worldwide, transcending time, so we have biblical principles to live and learn today.

Biblical connection

Paul's example is one we can learn from and see the impact. People of connection have on the world around them. Paul understood that organizations are "living, social organisms."[78] Paul, originally known as Saul, was an absolute zealot regarding enforcing the Law and eliminating all Christians (Acts 9:1–2). Saul knew every aspect of the law and, with it, would have seen the destruction of the Christian faith. He was also proud, arrogant, and determined, but Saul's life turned upside down when he encountered Jesus on the road to Damascus. Everything he thought he knew was exposed to the truth of Jesus, and he surrendered his entire life to Him, becoming Paul.

Paul's radical conversion and the instructions he received caused him to live connected with the heart of Jesus. He also had the task of training, correcting, and establishing the Christian culture. The core culture Paul built came from his history, nature, social experi-

---

[78] Schneider 2000, 25.

ences, and his perception of how to succeed.[79] He imparted wisdom and knowledge to those under his tutelage, gave them leadership authority, and sent Tychicus to Ephesus (Ephesians 6:21–22 NASB) and Timothy to Philippi (Philippians 2:19–23 NASB). Leaders act with wisdom when distributing leadership throughout an organization.[80] Paul developed leaders who would carry on the message of Jesus and the culture of Christianity when he was gone. Through Paul's leadership and instruction, Christianity has become an enduring institution.[81]

Throughout his teaching, Paul consistently developed his leaders and the relationships between the new believers, which is another way to think of people of connection. They shared a learning process that further set the Christian culture.[82] Focusing on a common goal and shared learning experiences strengthened the core values and beliefs, leading to generations of Christians following Paul's teaching and training. Paul's life and experiences show how one person of connection can cause change and influence in multiple locations, cultures, and generations.

In Romans 12:2 (NASB), Paul says,

> Do not be conformed to this world, but be
> transformed by the renewing of your mind, so
> that you may prove what the will of God is, that
> which is good and acceptable and perfect.

Paul was concerned with reinforcing the culture of the new church so that it would align with the guiding principles of Jesus. He was bringing in a change, a new way of believing, and the culture change shocked most people. A charismatic leader can change a culture with new beliefs and values.[83] Paul was this charismatic leader. When he was persecuting the church, he said he was the chief of

---

[79] Schneider 2000.
[80] Chatterjee 2006.
[81] Ibid.
[82] Schein and Schein 2016.
[83] Ibid.

zealots, a witness to the stoning of Stephen in Acts 7, and began persecuting the church in Acts 8. Paul put all his energy into persecuting the church. When he became a follower of Jesus, he put all his energy into preaching the gospel and establishing the culture of believers.

Paul also instructed his leaders in the power of the Holy Spirit, "who is from God, so that we may know the things freely given to us by God" (1 Corinthians 2:12 NASB). In 1 Corinthians 3 (NASB), Paul instructed followers of Jesus on the foundations for living. Paul taught and led with the assurance of the Holy Spirit. In 2 Timothy 4:1 (NASB), Paul named Timothy his immediate successor, providing believers with another person of connection as a leader in the Christian church. At that time, Paul knew his death was imminent. He gave clear guidance to Timothy to take up his charge and continue to preach the gospel of Jesus. When Paul passed his mantle to Timothy as successor, the new culture of Christianity needed to continue integrating the new identity, values, and procedures. Timothy's training and instruction from Paul were ingrained and detailed so Timothy could continue to train and teach others.

People of connection also look for the value in others, acknowledge their contributions, and celebrate their victories. Paul points out exhortation, mercy, diligence, and rejoicing in hope as actions and values add to believers' building up.[84] He focused on the positive actions of the believers, which was utterly different from focusing on the sins, as he did under the law. Paul contributed to the transformation of believers by reminding them of their value and how they can contribute to the body of believers.[85] Paul focused on bringing out the best in people and reminding them to look for the best in each other.

Global leaders also have this charge by providing people of connection with guidance, encouragement, and a sense of purpose and vision for success.[86] People of connection build strong relationships with others, connecting in positive ways that multiply the possibilities in each.

---

[84] Gillespie and Mann 2004.

[85] Cooper 2005.

[86] Gillespie and Mann 2004, Kouzes and Posner 2017.

People of Connection

Who you are

Does your leadership reflect your relationships with yourself and with God? Are you self-aware of who you are, what you have, and how to walk as "people of connection"? Are you intentional about cultivating positive relationships with others? What moral foundation, values, and morals do you live by?

Do you give your people of connection grace to learn and grow, make mistakes, and encourage them to refocus, try again, and become better than they think they are?

How you see God and who you think God is affects your perspective as a leader and people of connection.

What you have

You have a talent, purpose, passion, and calling inside of you that will impact the world for good. You have spiritual gifts that God gave you to change your world. We talked about the ripple effect. Do not despise small beginnings. Grow from the inside out.

How to walk in it

Live from the inside out. Be intentional with your connections to God and the people He brings into your life. Relationships are built on trust, empathy, and love. As you live from the inside out, you are an image bearer and light carrier of the living God. Do your internal values align with your external actions?

Scripture

> But the fruit of the Spirit is love, joy, peace, patience, kindness, goodness, faithfulness, gentleness, and self-control; against such things, there is no law. (Galatians 5:22 NASB)

But the fruit produced by the Holy Spirit within you is divine love in all its varied expressions: Joy that overflows, peace that subdues, patience that endures, kindness in action, a life full of virtue, faith that prevails, gentleness of heart and strength of spirit.

Never set the law above these qualities, for they are meant to be limitless. (Galatians 5:22 TPT)

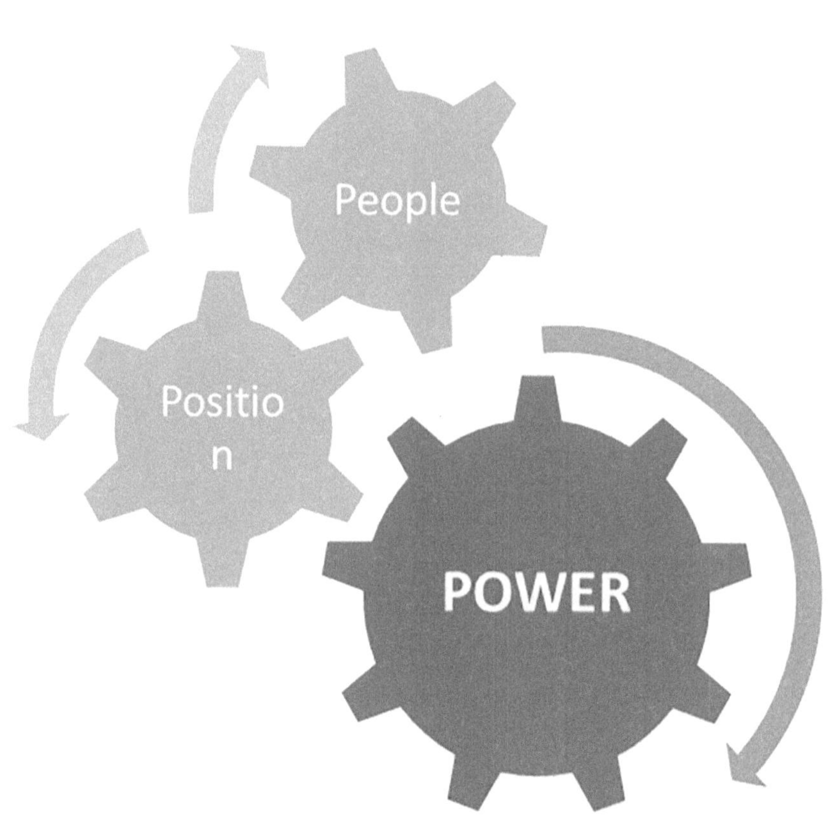
People
Positio
n
POWER

Power of Connection

Leadership points of connection involve power in one way or another. Interactions with others can build valuable and productive connections and encourage independent and innovative thoughts and ideas. Leaders who understand the power of connection know they can influence others through their actions and position of authority. Healthy relationships require trust that only comes from the intentional effort of character and authenticity, which relates to a leader's core values and beliefs. Networking with others through work and community builds powerful connections that can improve and build up individuals and places of influence. There is also a spiritual power of connection with God that uplifts and encourages us while enhancing our power of connection with people.

Leadership influence involves transformation through the power of connection.[87] Power is a force that is a part of our everyday selves, implicit in interpersonal relationships, present in organizational structure, within social relations, and between groups.[88] The connection between leader and follower builds on trust, communication, and a common purpose.[89] An organizational leader has two types of power: position and personal. Positional power derives

---

[87] Northouse 2019.

[88] Vince 2014.

[89] Northouse 2019.

from their office or rank within the organizational structure, whereas personal power comes from likeability and knowledge through their actions.[90] Leaders who use their influence positively and encouragingly demonstrate the idealized impact that benefits others.[91] Influential leaders should not use their position and authority to abuse or coerce others through cockiness or arrogance, leading to adverse outcomes.[92] The power of connection relies heavily on the leader's core values and beliefs that encourage authenticity, leading to positive transformation.

Core values and beliefs are ethical and moral guides that help individuals make decisions and shape leadership behavior.[93] Authenticity means living by your beliefs, standards, ethics, and ideals and communicating your beliefs in ways that characterize who you are.[94] Core values and beliefs empower leaders to make ethical and moral decisions that demonstrate authenticity and provide firm guidance in leadership philosophy.[95] Two of the United States Army values are selfless service and integrity. Selfless service means placing others first, as in servant leadership. Integrity is doing what is legally and morally right. Selfless service and integrity are core values leaders have that demonstrate a powerful connection to followers and set an example worthy of leadership.

Coach and mentor

Leaders can use the power of connection to inspire followers through inspirational motivation. Inspirational motivation combines energy, initiative, persistence, and vision to exceed performance outcomes and expectations and develop leadership potential.[96] Motivation is powerful, combining psychological and emotional

---

90 Ibid.
91 Sosik and Jung 2018.
92 Ibid.
93 Ibid.
94 Kouzes and Posner 2017.
95 Ibid.
96 Sosik and Jung 2018.

processes unique to individuals.[97] When the leader and follower connect, the leader learns what motivates the follower through positive transformation. Insightful coaching and the power of connection can help accomplish collective strategic change.[98] The power of connection multiplies and benefits the individual and the organization through coaching and mentoring.

Coaches and mentors are powerful points of connection, personally and professionally. Both relationships help an individual grow in ways that build performance and satisfaction. A coach's primary focus is on tasks and performance. Coaches can have fields of focus or specialties to get people where they need to be. Coaching specialties include life, health and wellness, executive, and leadership, to name a few. Coaches help guide clients toward specific goals, with positive changes extending beyond the coaching experience.[99] The characteristics of positive coaching include lasting developmental effects for the individual while meeting strategic organizational needs.[100] In addition, coaching produces lasting transformational change that influences people beyond coaching, which is the essence of a "power of connection." Collins challenges coaches to look at people from God's point of view, in which transformation is possible because of the potential He sees in them.[101] When coaches understand the power of connection, positive changes are possible.

Mentors have a similar power of connection, much like coaches. Mentors partner with mentees to share wisdom and knowledge, usually in a specific industry where they have expertise. The power of connection as a mentor or mentee is evident in the relationship between the two. Mentors help others climb to the new highest in career, skills, or abilities.[102] Mentors can analyze and assess performance, pointing out strengths and flaws that can enable growth and

---

[97] Engstrom 1976.
[98] Anderson 2005.
[99] Ibid.
[100] Ibid.
[101] Collins 2009.
[102] Witzel 2014.

success.[103] A mentor is a powerful connection willing to commit time and energy to guide growth and development.[104] Mentoring relationships take time and are best suited to teachable individuals ready to learn and grow.[105] The power of connection between mentor and mentee can be a source of transforming influence on each.

Better together

Group dynamics or team building is also affected by the power of connection. The power of connection causes increases through collaboration and networking. Ideas expand, generate solutions, and increase innovation. It requires effective communication. A leader's mission is to combine desires, skills, and energy to achieve a common goal.[106] Effective communication starts with the leader's perspective, values, and character.[107] The leader's ability to communicate effectively builds trust and meaning between leader and follower. Communication also contributes to organizational purpose by providing alignment, focus, and clarity that add depth and dimension to the organizational culture.[108] With effective communication, collaboration, and trust, the power of connection in groups or teams grows beyond the individual and solidifies the cohesiveness a team needs for success.

Communication

How the leader communicates is also essential in reinforcing the power of connection. One aspect of how to communicate effectively includes emotional intelligence. Emotional intelligence (EI) or emotional quotient (EQ) encompasses self-awareness, self-regulation, social skills, motivation, and empathy, which is why a leader's char-

---

[103] Kouzes and Posner 2017.
[104] Collins 2009.
[105] Gunn 2016, Pittenger and Heimann 2000.
[106] Engstrom 1976.
[107] Baldoni 2003.
[108] Anderson and Adams 2015.

acter is so important.[109] The leader's character comes from core values and beliefs, which help develop emotional intelligence, leading to effective communication, greater understanding, and increased productivity.[110] Effective communication supports the power of connection between leader and follower that builds trust, further enhancing group dynamics and team building.

Listening skills are also vital to effective communication. Not only do leaders have to get the message across, but they also must listen with purpose and empathy to questions and concerns. Effective communication impacts attitudes, well-being, and a willingness to put in more effort for the organization.[111] Communication is a two-way process of speaking, listening, and checking for understanding.[112] Active-listening skills bring sharing and clarification while developing connections that open new possibilities.[113] The best communication acknowledges and understands the feelings of others in a way that builds bridges in the relationship.[114] Bridges are powerful connections that help expand relationships, overcome obstacles, and provide a path for others to follow. When leaders look at power from a bridge perspective, it changes their mindset from "power over" to "power with" connection.

Bridges are two-way, and the power of connection is two-way. The military uses the phrase "I got your six," meaning I have your back and protect you from behind. As one soldier moves forward, their battle buddy is right behind. Soldiers learn the power of connection in training that builds relationships. During combat, soldiers rely on each other through the power of connection to accomplish missions and keep each other alive. The power of connection soldiers have with one another is a two-way bridge built with dedication, trust, and consistency. It is part of the military culture to build successful bridges and teams. It is also what connects veterans for life. As

---

[109] Goleman 1995.
[110] Northouse 2019.
[111] De Lange and Mulder 2022.
[112] Baldoni 2003.
[113] Center for Creative Leadership 2019.
[114] Engstrom 1976.

people discover the power of connection, their personal and community growth increases positive outcomes. Positive personal and communal change only comes from "power with" connections.

Leaders who focus on their positional power can lose sight of their relationship with others. A leader who displays power through cockiness, arrogance, and overconfidence based on position rather than relationships quickly erodes their influence with followers and associates.[115] The capacity to connect transcends positional power, especially when a leader understands that growth and development thrive in healthy relationships.[116] Healthy communication is essential to healthy relationships, creativity and productivity, better-performing teams, and ethical behaviors.[117] Leaders must understand the difference between positional power and the influence that builds a bridge of trust with followers, even without position or authority.[118] Communication is critical to building the bridge or power of connection.

Authentic leadership

Authentic leadership is a style that uses the power of connection in multiple ways to cultivate trust and build relationships with the power of connection. Authentic leaders emphasize life experiences critical to leadership development.[119] Life experiences are relatable, meaning similar life experiences or situations can help leaders connect to others. Leaders can use life experiences that foster growth and resilience to encourage that same in followers and associates. Growth relationships are not in constant connection but connect and reconnect all the time.[120] Resilient, authentic leaders understand that connection/reconnection is part of growth, self-awareness, and self-development.

---

[115] Sosik and Jung 2017.
[116] Banks 2011.
[117] Mercader et al. 2021.
[118] Sosik and Jung 2018.
[119] Northouse 2019.
[120] Banks 2011.

One example comes from the army. Soldiers transfer to new duty stations every few years to change jobs or accept promotions. With every new duty station comes new team members and leaders. Soldiers learn to adapt quickly for two reasons: the joint mission and values of the army and the shared life experiences that come with serving the army. The connection-reconnection process is negative and positive, which helps build resilience in the soldiers and their relationships with fellow soldiers.[121]

Organizations that support and promote creativity in leadership and employees build trust and commitment leading to growth strategies.[122] In addition, certain leadership styles that encourage creativity lead to effective teams that produce desirable outcomes at multiple levels.[123] Howard Schultz, of Starbucks fame, recognized the need for creative intelligence at Starbucks when he hired Wright Massey as vice president of design.[124] Massey's skill in creativity and strategic planning led the design team to develop a comprehensive store design that exceeded Schultz's expectations.[125] Schultz displayed authentic leadership traits by remaining true to his vision of Starbucks while allowing his creative team to present innovative designs for Starbucks stores. As an authentic leader, Schultz encouraged enthusiasm that promoted creative ideas and solve problems.[126] In addition, Schultz set clear goals and guidance that aligned with his vision that influenced the creative activity of his design team.[127]

Authentic leaders like Schultz can influence their employees' creativity through an organizational culture that welcomes and encourages creative ideas and innovative solutions. In addition, they can offer training in creative problem-solving or content-based skills that further creative development.[128] Encouraging ingenuity among

---

[121] Banks 2011.

[122] Sosik and Jung 2018.

[123] Northouse 2019, Sosik and Jung 2018.

[124] Schultz 1997.

[125] Ibid.

[126] Semedo, Coelho, and Ribeiro 2016.

[127] Shalley and Gilson 2004.

[128] Ibid.

all levels of employees displays authentic leadership that shows followers that their contributions are essential to organizational success.[129] In addition, communication and listening are necessary components of authentic leadership.[130]

Authentic leaders can also develop a powerful connection with their followers. They can help create authentic communities by their example and by engaging others with the strength of their commitment to authenticity.[131] Authentic leaders live from the inside out, from their values and moral decision-making, and personal experience. They also admit when they are wrong. I recall one instance when I argued with one of my soldiers and said some things in anger that I regretted. Even though much of what I said was right, some things I said were wrong in my attitude and tone. It took much humility for me to go to my soldier later to apologize and ask how I could help restore the relationship. Although leaders want to be right 100 percent of the time and never have to apologize, authentic leaders know when they are wrong, when to apologize, and then take steps to restore the relationship.

Authentic leadership is a matter of credibility and trust, with the expectation that leaders are fallible, and their credibility comes from acknowledging they have weaknesses and make mistakes.[132] Time and experience also enhance credibility, but grace gives compassion to fallible leaders who recognize and learn from their mistakes.[133] People look for leaders who communicate character traits that genuinely represent who they are.[134] The power of connection through authentic leadership comes from the interpersonal process between leaders and followers. An authentic leader connects with others, creates a reciprocal relationship built on trust, and promotes self-development.[135] The point of connection between an authentic

---

[129] Engstrom 1976, Northhouse 2019.
[130] Kouzes and Posner 2017.
[131] Collins 2009.
[132] Anderson and Adams 2015.
[133] Ibid.
[134] Kouzes and Posner 2017.
[135] Anderson and Adams 2015, Northhouse 2019.

leader and a follower supports inspiration, purpose, and passion in both leader and follower.

Transformational leadership

Transformational leaders also seek to engage and connect with followers, which increase motivation and morality in the leader and follower.[136] Transformational leaders value the power of connection with their followers, raising personal and professional expectations and goals, and encouraging creativity and innovation.[137] The transformational leader can incorporate creative intelligence, cultivated through creative thinking and problem-solving, encouraging intelligent thought and innovative ideas. A leader's role in follower creativity is evident in the relationship, the organizational climate, and job characteristics. The power of connection between the leader and follower increases the creative capacity, generating better ideas and solutions.

The power of connection to transformational leaders involves the four factors that motivate followers to do more than expected: idealized influence, inspirational motivation, intellectual stimulation, and idealized consideration.[138] Idealized influence is the strong moral character of the leader, providing followers with a role model to emulate.[139] The power of connection in idealized influence is the leader's example of positive, moral character traits that demonstrate integrity, honor, and ethics that followers can see, respect, and trust. A leader's inspirational motivation communicates high standards and expectations to the followers, encouraging and pushing them to achieve more than they thought possible through a shared vision and teamwork.[140] When team members work together and align with an organization's visions, the power of connection brings alignment and focus, achieving more together.

---

[136] Northouse 2019.
[137] García-Morales et al. 2012.
[138] Northouse 2019.
[139] Ibid.
[140] Ibid.

Moreover, intellectual stimulation adds creativity and innovation, which broaden perspectives, encourage problem-solving, and challenge followers and team members to think creatively.[141] With individualized consideration, the leader supports the follower through coaching or mentoring, guiding, and assisting the follower with personal and professional development.[142] The power of connection with individualized consideration results in the follower fully realizing their value and achieving more than they thought possible.

Servant leadership

As a power of connection, servant leadership is a relationship between leaders and followers rooted in love.[143] Because its foundation is love, servant leaders focus on the individual rather than the organization.[144] Servant leaders meet organizational goals and objectives by empowering individuals through servant leaders. Biblical leaders demonstrate leadership by responding to a call to action with a personal, flexible approach that meets the community's needs.[145] Servant leadership is a spiritual calling that proceeds from inside the leader and manifests outside.[146] Servant leadership foundations applied internally result in leadership growth while serving others. Serving others is a high call and a powerful connection to others.

Biblical leadership principles transcend culture and time and apply to leadership challenges experienced in all areas of life.[147] From a biblical perspective, servant-leadership principles and traits place individuals and relationships ahead of the organization or community, not excluding the organization's goals. Aligning individual and organizational goals and objectives creates a mutually beneficial and powerful dynamic relationship. Paul's example of servant leadership

---

[141] Ibid.

[142] Ibid.

[143] Patterson 2003.

[144] Ibid.

[145] Agosto 2005.

[146] Crowther 2018.

[147] Bell 2014.

applied to every community and culture he encountered. Biblical servant-leader principles transcend time to present-day leaders, organizations, and communities. When servant leaders empower individuals, they can add significance to the organization with internal values, principles, and relationships. Organizational culture and context also influence servant leadership in applying external manifestations.[148] Actions appropriate to the organization or industry are essential considerations in servant leadership.

When actioning the principles of servant leadership, the outcomes include personal growth and performance, organizational performance, and societal impact.[149] The results of servant leadership empower followers and maximize their potential. In turn, empowered followers contribute to enhanced organizational performance, positively impacting society. Servant-leadership principles are, in a sense, perpetual because they do not stop with the individual. The results affect many areas of society and culture.

With a selfless mindset, servant leaders carry influence in any area and industry. The servant leader focuses on the individual and leads them in growth and development, positively impacting the organization.[150] Servant leaders operate from knowing who they are; their purpose is to serve and lead. Servant leadership is a calling that proceeds from the inside out.[151] Service comes from the heart, from a position of love to the outside, demonstrated through service. When the servant also leads, it comes from love and a desire to uplift, provoke, and propel followers to their best selves. In Mark 10:43 (TPT), Jesus says, "You are to lead by a different model. If you want to be the greatest one, live as one called to serve others." Jesus's example was of servant leadership rather than the example of leaders who ruled by oppression.

Servant leaders also apply listening and compassion skills to build trusting relationships with followers to empower them.[152]

---

[148] Northhouse 2019.

[149] Ibid.

[150] Coetzer, Bussin, and Geldenhuys 2017.

[151] Bell and Habel 2010.

[152] Coetzer, Bussin, and Geldenhuys 2017.

Empowerment requires continuous growth and development by encouraging and activating individual talent.[153] Servant leaders also help followers develop a vision and align thinking and outcomes that help fulfill the vision.[154] Combing humility and behaviors encourages action and efficacy.[155] Humility shows a willingness to place others ahead of self, giving support and credit to uplift and inspire.[156]

Servant leadership proceeds from knowing who you are in Christ and serving from that position. Jesus lived from the inside out, knowing who His Father was and operating in His mission and calling. In John 8:28 (NASB), Jesus says He does nothing on His own initiative but only what He sees the Father doing. The virtues of servant leadership must be practiced through relationships, just as Jesus had a relationship with the Father. Jesus modeled the way by defining, affirming, and aligning actions with shared values.[157]

When servant-leadership values are defined and lived from the inside out, servant leaders have a foundation to communicate and collaborate with followers.[158] However, because relationships are dynamic, servant leadership is not guaranteed effective, particularly when the leader's and follower's values do not align.[159] Therefore, the servant leader must define and apply values that help reinforce the power of connection with followers. In addition, servant leaders emphasize the importance of placing followers first, being honest, and developing long-term relationships.[160]

Paul's letters are examples of servant leadership in the New Testament that show his priorities were sharing the gospel, building relationships with his followers, and building a community of believers. In Philippians 2:3–4, Paul encourages the Philippians to regard others as more important than self and to look out for personal inter-

---

[153] Ibid.

[154] Bell and Habel 2010.

[155] Sousa and Van Dierendonck 2017.

[156] Ibid.

[157] Kouzes and Posner 2017.

[158] Ibid.

[159] Mizzell and Huizing 2018.

[160] Northouse 2019.

ests and the interests of others. Humility and selflessness are two qualities Paul emphasizes, which also align with servant leadership. Servant leaders are revolutionary. Servant leadership is paradoxical in that leaders serve first and then lead, working for the good of an individual's growth and development. Secondary goals are for the good of the organization and the community. As revolutionaries, servant leaders can affect organizational culture and social change, becoming points of connection that bring others together. To create a high performance culture, you must bring others whose values align with the organization.[161] A servant-leader culture can be a high performance culture with a good alignment of values and points of connection.[162]

In addition, senior leaders in an organization can affect the culture through consistently upholding and actioning servant-leadership values,[163] thereby modeling the way. One description of servant leadership includes three stages. The first stage is preparation through developing internal character and a proper worldview in love.[164] The second stage involves leading from a calling and a purpose. The third stage is creating a legacy of leadership. Each stage of leadership growth builds on the previous by learning to lead from an internal calling rather than a position.[165] As leaders become confident in their values and know their calling and purpose, they empower followers to grow and develop, leading to a servant-leadership culture, thereby forming a legacy of servant leadership.

An essential issue contemporary servant leaders face is the understanding that we serve God by leading others in love. Psalm 23 shows God leading and serving us because of His great love for us, not because of anything we have done or accomplished. He does it because He is love—also called "steward leadership," which is caring, loving, and leading from God's vision for us.[166] Another description is spiritual leadership, in which God gives leaders a vision to steward

---

[161] Kouzes and Posner 2017.
[162] Crowther 2018.
[163] Ibid.
[164] Ibid.
[165] Sun 2013.
[166] Rodin 2013.

and carry.[167] As servant leaders, we can impact people, organizations, and communities.[168] Every leader in the Old Testament began with God as the true leader, who gave them a vision, which they stewarded and led others to fulfill the vision.

Servant leadership qualities include listening, empathy, healing, awareness, persuasion, conceptualization, foresight, stewardship, commitment to the growth of people, and building community.[169] Jesus exemplified and demonstrated these qualities through relationships with His disciples and the general public. His life was an example of servant leadership.

Servant leadership is also a virtuous, internal, or spiritual theory.[170] Some of the characteristics of servant leadership can be learned, such as listening, awareness, persuasion, or foresight.[171] Others take on a deeper meaning when combined with the internal characteristics of empathy, healing, and commitment to the growth of people. The serving leader considers the whole individual, with wants, needs, and desires, while guiding and challenging the individual to grow.[172] The foundation of servant leadership is love, which is a power of connection.

Jesus's servant-leadership model was direct: "Greater love has no one than this, that one lay down his life for his friends" (John 15:13 NASB). Jesus was the archetype of servant leadership. His direct relationship and connection with Father God was the model His followers could see and emulate. Jesus's example was perfect and showed the power of connection to God. Jesus reminded His disciples that to be first, you must sacrifice yourself for those in need[173] (Mark 10:45 NASB). Jesus presented the theory and principles of servant leadership to His disciples, who then put His principles into action, as in Acts 2:45, when the followers of Jesus shared with those in need.

---

[167] Bell 2014.

[168] Coetzer, Bussin, and Geldenhuys 2017.

[169] Spears 2010.

[170] Patterson 2003.

[171] Spears 2010.

[172] Crowther 2018.

[173] Agosto 2005.

Paul's servant-leadership model developed after encountering Jesus on the road to Damascus. Paul said in Galatians 1:11–12 that he received the gospel directly from Jesus. His apostolic task was to preach the gospel of Jesus to the Gentiles. After his conversion, Paul preached the gospel for three years before he met the disciples in Jerusalem.

Paul also traveled extensively, encountering many cultures, tribes, and nations. Everywhere he went, Paul taught with authority given to him by Jesus. His message included service before self and addressed issues and concerns in the context of the culture. When Paul discusses the gifts of the Spirit in 1 Corinthians 12, he reminds the Corinthians that gifts are for the members of the body, not to glorify themselves but in service to one another. Leadership as a relational and community process[174] exhibits the power of connection for the good of all.

Paul also included self-transformation in pursuit of personal growth while serving others. He encouraged the followers of Jesus to serve each other, those with whom they shared the gospel. Paul demonstrated practical actions of servant leadership that others could model up to the contemporary church and organizations.

Modern leaders can learn insights and principles from Paul that apply to organizational ethics, values, and vision to create a shared service goal within the organization and the community.[175] Servant-leadership principles can be taught and developed in a contemporary organization.[176]

Servant leadership is more than completing acts of service. It is important to remember that servant leadership starts with choosing to serve and then lead.[177] Service places the needs of others before self, just as Jesus put the needs of humanity before Himself. Servant leadership also includes leading others into growth and development. Leadership practices encourage followers to model the way, inspire a shared vision, challenge the process, enable others to act, and encour-

---

[174] Bell 2014.
[175] Ibid.
[176] Northouse 2019.
[177] Greenleaf 1977.

age the heart to become powerful connections that work toward a common good.[178]

Effective communication is vital to the servant leader–follower relationship.[179] Research indicates a correlation between servant-leadership communication to followers and positive connections, job satisfaction, organizational commitment, and lower job turnover.[180] Humility is also essential to servant leadership, especially in the hierarchy of organizational relationships.[181] A servant leader's actions with humility can influence followers' behavior in demonstrating qualities and actions of servant-leadership components. In addition, servant leaders can empower followers to think, behave, act, control work, and make decisions that encourage ownership of themselves and their contributions to the organization.[182] Servant leaders who empower followers through foresight, persuasion, awareness, and stewardship impact individual and organizational performance.[183] Jesus clarifies that true leadership is grounded in love, which must issue in service.[184]

In the letter to the Corinthian church, Paul covers various topics. First Corinthians 13, considered the love chapter, expounds on the foundation of love that strengthens the servant-leadership model. Leadership is grounded in love.[185] First Corinthians 13:4–7 lists the actions of love: patience, kindness, forgiving, truth, forbearance, belief, hope, and endurance. The actions of a servant leader support followers with love from the heart. Servant leaders desire to serve others, help them achieve goals, and become more than they thought possible.[186]

---

[178] Kouzes and Posner 2017.

[179] Sloan, Mikkelson, and Wilkinson 2020.

[180] Ibid.

[181] Sousa and Van Dierendonck 2015.

[182] Murari and Gupta 2012.

[183] Ibid.

[184] Enstrom 1976.

[185] Bell 2014.

[186] Whittington et al. 2005.

Paul also discusses growth and maturity in 1 Corinthians 13:11. Servant leaders use experience, maturity, and life lessons to impart wisdom and knowledge to followers to assist their intellectual, spiritual, and emotional growth. As followers grow and mature, their contributions add value to the organization.[187] The followers' learning, growing, and developing process is more valuable to servant leaders than attaining power and position.

The agape love Paul describes is practical for transforming lives, reconciling relationships, and producing good fruit individually and corporately.[188] Paul reminded the Corinthian church that their actions and decisions influenced believers and unbelievers. Paul's reminder applies to servant leadership today. Servant leaders who teach, train, and mentor with love set aside selfish gain and ambition to help develop followers and influence the next generation of servant leaders.[189] Organizations that recognize and incorporate servant-leadership training help nurture emotional intelligence, ethical decision-making, and empowering skills.[190] Practical application of servant leadership founded on love bears fruit from the individual to the organization and surrounding community.

Contemporary servant leaders must also follow Paul's leadership techniques when leading others. Leaders walking in authenticity and integrity cannot be afraid to correct followers when needed, always with love and encouragement. Authenticity is not something exclusive to the church or any other organization. Servant leaders carry these qualities and live them from the inside out. It is a way of life, built on a foundation of love in Christ Jesus, that servant leaders walk out and demonstrate no matter where they go and whom they encounter. Leadership is a relational process,[191] having less to do with position and more with community and relationships God has placed in our path.

---

[187] Northouse 2019.

[188] Bell 2014.

[189] Crowther 2018.

[190] Northouse 2019.

[191] Bell 2014.

Servant leadership is a lifelong process that defines a legacy and trains the next generation of servant leaders. Excellence in Christian leadership as a process that requires constant evaluation, correction, and improvement.[192] The process is what Paul describes in the letters to the Corinthians. In 1 Corinthians 9:24–27, Paul speaks of the process involving self-control, discipline, training, direction, and vision. The servant-leader process also depends on those four categories to develop the leader within and then pass that process to followers.

Better together

As mentors, servant leaders combine organizational-specific training with relationships and follower development.[193] The mentorship process helps change lives to reflect love, care, and concern to the mentor.[194] When followers become leaders, they, in turn, change lives with the love, care, and concern they were shown.[195] Mentorship for the servant leader also includes a continuous process of internal improvement. Mentoring followers through self-improvement, goals, foresight, skill building, and community relationships also empowers followers.[196]

With empowerment also comes responsibility and accountability. Paul discusses accountability in 2 Corinthians 13:1–3. He reminds the believers again not to tolerate sin and that even through weakness, the power of God within strengthens us. Paul's example applies to servant leaders and followers for accountability. Servant leaders are accountable for their actions, just as followers are accountable for their actions.[197] Accountability helps build the relationship between leader and follower while encouraging each other to uphold values and morals. Accountability helps leaders and followers maintain excellence throughout the leadership.

---

[192] Engstrom 1976.
[193] Pearson 2012.
[194] Whittington et al. 2005.
[195] Ibid.
[196] Murari and Gupta 2012.
[197] Northouse 2019.

Unity and collaboration are significant in leadership. The promotion of unity and collaboration begins with a vision. Leaders challenge followers to imagine exciting and ennobling possibilities by sharing a common vision.[198] When Paul speaks of the spiritual gifts in 1 Corinthians 12, he describes the body of Christ as having varieties of gifts but the same Spirit. This Spirit binds Christians in unity and collaboration in the love of Christ. When the church operates in the unity of the Spirit, it can achieve more than arguing over what gift or who is the greatest.

In organizations outside the church, unity and collaboration point to a shared vision. Servant leaders can help provide the vision of service for the betterment of followers, the organization, and the community. Moreover, servant leadership uniquely and positively impacts subordinates, teams, and organizations.[199] Servant leadership brings about a sense of accomplishment, positive emotions, and innovative ideas through powerful connections.

Unity and collaboration are sorely needed in the United States of America right now. We have lost the vision of America as a beacon of freedom in Christ, espousing a division of thought, culture, and purpose. As servant leaders and Christians, we are responsible for serving others and building followers for a better future, but we also have to stand firm in the Christian principles and ideas from Scripture. We are to be in the world but not of the world.

Many people do not know their identity and have lost their way. We need to clearly remember Paul's words to the Corinthians that the same God works in and through all things, and we are all members of one body with one Spirit in Christ Jesus. Agape love is the superpower of connection. When you connect with others in love, as in servant leadership, the richness and depth of your relationship expand. First Corinthians 13:13 (TPT) says, "Until then, three things remain: faith, hope, and love—yet love surpasses them all." So above all else, let love be the beautiful prize for which you

---

[198] Kouzes and Posner 2017.
[199] Lan, Xia, and Yang 2021.

run. Love meets the needs of individuals, connects us with God, and never fails.

Leading soldiers

As a military leader, I had positional power based on rank and structure within my organization. When you join the military, you learn the rank structure and positional power. The military organizational structure upholds discipline, maintains a chain of command, and provides formal communication channels. The military structure is vital to its mission to defend the United States.[200] The power of connection within the military is built into the structure. The United States Army command structure details connections from the headquarters department of the army to all subordinate commands. The chain-of-command structure provides a clear communication path from the top level down to the individual soldier and vice versa.

The power of connection for a military organization keeps it functioning and orderly and helps build the culture and community within units. A camaraderie exists between soldiers built on mutual training, respect, and shared experiences. The power of connection reinforces the military, saying, "I've got your six," meaning I will look out for you as you look out for me. The power of connection is essential to the military, just as it is in business organizations, churches, and community leaders.

The power of connection also exists between generations of service members, who acknowledge the service and sacrifice of the former and current service members. When I retired from the US Army after twenty-one years of service, there was a sense of loss, a disconnect from the soldiers I served with. I went from constantly working—with daily meetings, reports, activities, and conversations—to a complete stop of everything. I felt that the "power of connection" was gone. There was a sense of loss of purpose and mission. However, I chose a new purpose and mission that includes plugging into the

---

[200] US Army, n.d.

power of connection within my community through veterans, volunteering, and working with small businesses. The power of my new points of connection helped to redefine my purpose and mission after military service.

Nonlinear power of connection

The power of connection is not linear. It works through multiple people and in various directions. The power of connection is a multiplying effect, energizing and strengthening people. The power of connection adds value to relationships and helps bridge gaps in business and communities, bringing others into a collaborative network who can exchange ideas and knowledge. It is part of a global leadership mindset that encourages creativity, curiosity, and engagement with others to build emotional connections, cultural awareness, and appreciation.[201] Connection invites others to participate in life's adventures, sharing experiences and ideas that inspire discussion, ideas, and perspectives.

When you are in a leadership position, you can connect with others in ways that empower you and your followers, peers, and colleagues. My friend John is an entrepreneur who owns several companies, holds multiple board positions, and is an investor in people. His newest project is a nonprofit community coffee shop. The inspiration for the coffee shop came from a connection John had with a priest whose desire was a meeting place for young people to gather, share ideas and friendships, and get to know each other over coffee.

The priest passed away before realizing his dream. With the power of connection, John carried on the dream and established a place for students to learn about the power of connection. John's coffee shop is also a meeting place for church groups, veterans, and others looking for points of connection in and around their community. People of connection and power of connection multiply in ways leading to meaningful outcomes guided by a higher purpose.

---

[201] Cseh, Davis, and Khilji 2012.

Power of Connection

Who you are

How does the power of connection apply to you? Who you are is where your power of connection lies. If you are a parent, your power of connection is with your child, to raise them to know the power of connection that values the relationship between parent and child. If you are a leader, your power of connection is with your followers, challenging them to more excellent outcomes and purpose. The most profound and authentic power of connection comes from God. Even if you feel alone and powerless, when you understand the power of connection with God, you know who you are within.

What you have

The power of connection is what you have within you that desires a close relationship with others. You have creative and innovative ideas that need the power of connection to multiply and change the world for good. When you connect with God through the life, death, and resurrection of Jesus, you have a spiritual connection that is a powerful source of life and light. You have God's love, the most extraordinary power of connection.

How to walk in it

Living a virtuous life from the inside out requires the power of connection only Jesus provides. You become a different person, a leader who places others above yourself. Walking in the power of connection helps you move into maturity, discernment, and vision moving from "power over" to "power with" others.

Scriptures

In Him, you have been made extravagantly
rich in every way. You have been endowed with

a wealth of inspired utterance and the riches that come from your intimate knowledge of Him. For the reality of the truth of Christ is seen among you and strengthened through your experience of Him. (1 Corinthians 1:5–6 TPT)

So now wrap your heart tightly around the hope within us, knowing that God keeps His promises! Discover creative ways to encourage others and to motivate them toward acts of compassion, doing beautiful works as expressions of love. (Hebrews 10:23–24 TPT)

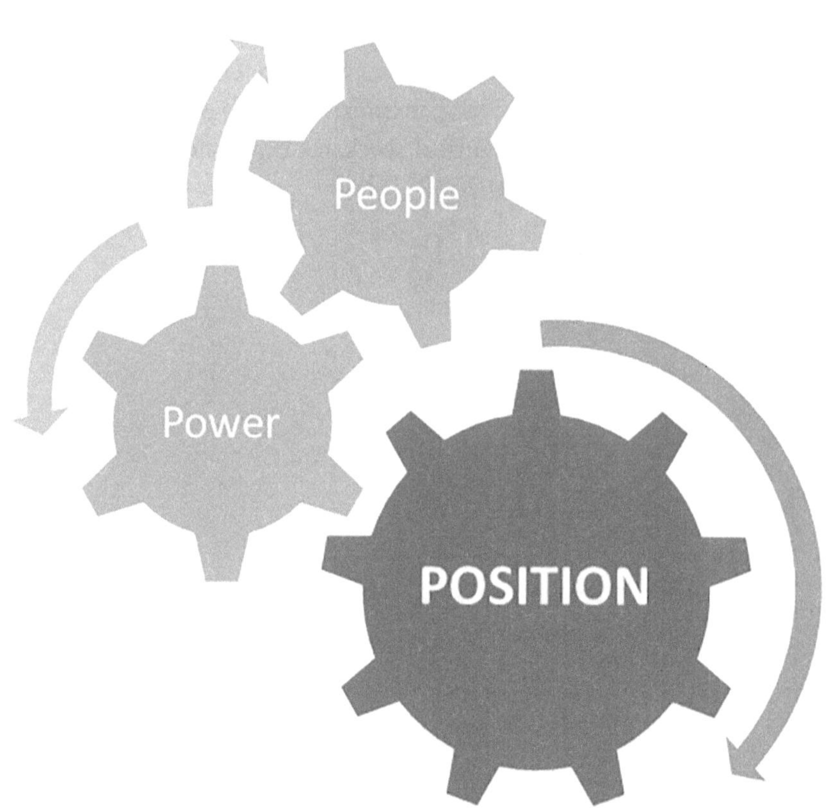

People
Power
POSITION

CHAPTER 3

Position of Connection

Position of connection is where you are in life, in work, in your family—any area that connects you with people who influence, teach, train, or encourage. Positions are connections with others. Your position can be CEO, manager, counselor, server, or pastor. However, titles are not the only positions of connection. Your position in the community may be as a first responder, military service member, volunteer, or any position that connects you with people. Networking is a kind of position of connection. A network connection can bring about new opportunities or introduce you to people you may not have met otherwise. Your position can place you in the company of people who bring you to a higher level of professional or personal development. When you are in a better position, you can connect with others to bring them to a higher position. For example, your position as a leader is where you can affect change, make decisions, or provide a service.

Leaders within an organization are positions of power by the organizational structure, assigned leadership, and emergent leadership.[202] Military leaders are assigned leadership positions according to rank and unit structure. The legitimacy of power in formal organizations is accepting an office as a right of legitimate power.[203]

---

[202] Northouse 2019.
[203] Raven and French 1958.

Examples of assigned leadership positions include CEO, vice president, and department manager. Assigned leadership is a position of connection recognized through organizational structure.

The US Army structure is an example of a well-planned and structured organization based on rank and position that builds on multiple organizational levels. The individual soldier is a team member with a team leader. Teams comprise squads with a squad leader, squads make up platoons with a platoon leader, and platoons form a company with one company commander and one first sergeant. Each level has a leadership position, giving the person in that position command and control authority.

As a leader in a position of authority, the connection between the leader and followers is essential. Organizational hierarchy utilizing structure provides authority to the person in the position. For organizations such as the military, the system is vital to maintaining discipline, assigning tasks and responsibilities, and keeping general order. Positional leaders also plan operations, make financial decisions, and are accountable to various interests, like stakeholders and constituents. The position of connection through positional leadership helps maintain order and focus on organizational objectives.

Team leaders can connect with each person and learn what motivates and inspires them. The small team size allows individuals to get to know one another, how they think, and how they can build a strong team. Leaders who connect emotionally to team members can transform them through encouragement, inspiration, guidance, and motivation.[204] Teams that work together for a long time can form a cohesive unit that functions together quickly and confidently.[205] Northouse stated that communication skills are essential as they allow a new leader to learn confidence and interact with others, creating a position of connection with team members.[206]

Another type of leader is an emergent leader. This person is perceived as a leader regardless of organizational position or title.[207]

---

[204] Momeny and Gourgues 2019.
[205] Kouzes and Posner 2017.
[206] Northouse 2019.
[207] Ibid.

Charismatic emergent leaders exhibit positive communication behaviors such as verbal skills, innovation, flexibility, curiosity, and empathy while drawing people to them. Traits like intelligence, self-confidence, determination, integrity, and sociability draw others to them in a workable relationship.[208] Although an emergent leader does not lead from a structured position, their qualities and interaction with a specific working group place them in a position of connection that influences others.

Emergent leaders may also have a position within an organization, but their influence extends beyond the structural role. Billy Graham was one such leader. His position of connection as an itinerant evangelist extended globally, resulting in crusades with hundreds of thousands of attendees and relationships with many people, including American presidents and other world leaders. Billy Graham's passionate communication style reinforced his position of connection that resonated through in-person events and broadcast media.

Communication

Emotions make emotional intelligence necessary for leaders and followers as a part of communication.[209] Individuals with emotional intelligence are self-aware and have self-control, self-discipline, and self-improvement. Leaders should encourage followers to learn and practice emotional intelligence that develops maturity and connection with others.[210] Emotional intelligence aids in productive communication when leaders and followers can engage in conversations and dialogue and share information rather than hoarding it in a communication silo.[211] Shared information through mutually beneficial communication breaks down barriers and assists with conflict resolution, further enhancing the value of the position of connection.

---

[208] Ibid.
[209] Avolio et al. 2004.
[210] Ibid.
[211] Zhou and George 2003.

Within organizations, communication silos occur when groups or teams, intentionally or unintentionally, hoard information or keep groups separate. Communication silos break down connections to coworkers and communication between leaders and followers, which could encourage conflicts within the organization.[212] Within the silo, team members focus inward and rely solely on those team members for all information, ideas, and guidance.

Silos can be detrimental to decisions outside that need that information or the team members' input.[213] For example, in a recent study on public health partnerships, communication silos affected knowledge exchange, hindering trust and decision-making.[214] The study also suggested that silos could assist in knowledge-sharing processes that could benefit partnerships. Leadership guidance as a position of connection is necessary for well-managed silos.[215] Leaders can be conduits as a position of connection, ensuring communication remains open between silos.

Leaders must also be bridge builders when communication silos exist.[216] The leader's function is to move the organization toward its mission and purpose while upholding the values of the organization. Communication silos should be recognized and acknowledged as potential barriers to effective communication, particularly when reinforcing the visions and purpose of the whole organization.[217] However, positive leverage can be used in existing silos to fill in information gaps if leaders understand how and when to cross the communication gaps.

Positions of connection also allow leaders to influence change within an organization or a body of constituents. Influence stems from the ability to effectively communicate the leader's vision or ideas for cultural transformation to others.[218] The position of connection

---

[212] Johnson, Grove, and Clark 2018.
[213] Brown, O'Connell, and Yoder 2018.
[214] Johnson, Grove, and Clarke 2018.
[215] Ibid.
[216] Brown, O'Connell, and Yoder 2018.
[217] Niall and Jiang 2017.
[218] Madestam and Falkman 2017.

as a change leader can manage the evolution of culture through stages of growth.[219] Communication, cultural intelligence, and emotional intelligence work together in leadership to build relationships, convey meaning, and provide an intentional direction.[220] A leader's position of connection creates opportunities to serve and build up new leaders.[221] A leader's best communication shows an understanding of the self, the individuals receiving the message, and the culture of the sender and recipient.[222] Combining emotional and cultural intelligence with precise communication results in a well-delivered message sympathetic to the listener.

The rumor mill, watercooler gossip, and break room chatter are connotations of informal communication. Organizations rely on formal communication through leaders and coworkers to share information, give direction and guidance, and disseminate policy or procedure. When formal communication is lacking, informal communication fills in the gaps.[223] Informal communication is more relaxed and rapid, like the proverbial grapevine with branches everywhere.[224] When examining informal communication in an organization, the negativity, rumors, and gossip that managers must address can detract from daily business and cause problems between individuals, teams, and management.[225] Management's influence over the grapevine depends on acknowledging its influence and exerting control over the rumor mill.[226]

The problem with the grapevine is its informal nature and lack of clarity and truth. Misinformation spreads like wildfire and can cause a breakdown in relationships or teams.[227] Believing misinformation can derail negotiations and productivity and cause dis-

---

[219] Schein and Schein 2016.
[220] Felício, Meidutė, and Kyvik 2016.
[221] Williams et al. 2017.
[222] Kyvik 2018.
[223] Erden 2013.
[224] Crampton, Hodge, and Mishra 1998.
[225] Banerjee and Singh 2015.
[226] Ibid.
[227] Crampton, Hodge, and Mishra 1998.

tractions. Because of the negativity bias everyone has, it is easier to believe lousy information and share it with others in the workplace.[228] Listening to one side of a conversation, hearing only a part of the story, and disclosing information outside the intended audience lead to assumptions and wrong conclusions and slows productivity. The misinformation spread may cause division or lead individuals to make spontaneous poor decisions with negative consequences.

Leaders within the organization are responsible for interacting with employees regularly, sharing information as needed, and communicating with employees.[229] Employees are responsible for sharing information responsibly and asking questions for clarification or guidance when necessary.[230] Communication solves many problems. Communication is essential to keep everyone informed and balanced so people have what they need to do the job and share workplace information.[231] Sharing information and communicating clearly and appropriately enhances the working environment, brings desired outcomes, and creates a positive informed culture.[232] Employees will not have to stop at the watercooler to hear what is happening in the organization.

Communication in leadership changes depending on the situation. Four types of leadership are expert, visionary, coach, and transformer.[233] Leaders need flexibility and agility when interacting with followers as a position of connection.[234] Leadership should come from a place of expertise, connected with compassion, appeal, and accountability. Continuous leadership development involves self-improvement and relationship improvement among peers and followers.[235] Although most leaders have a naturally specific style, leadership communication is not a one-size-fits-all approach. The leader needs

---

[228] Zhou, Liu, Su, and Xu 2019.
[229] Banerjee and Singh 2015.
[230] Kouzes and Posner 2017.
[231] Ibid.
[232] Schein and Schein 2016.
[233] Baldoni 2003.
[234] Northouse 2019.
[235] Kouzes and Posner 2017.

to learn and understand followers, not to change to suit everyone but to develop productive relationships with followers.

Baldoni states that the leadership communication style varies.[236] Leaders need to know their audience, how to connect, and what appeals to the audience. The purpose of the message contributes to the communication style.[237] Since the message can vary, the communication style can vary.

Emotional intelligence

Emotional intelligence and cultural awareness work together in the effective leader to guide followers in meeting the organization's mission. Leadership communication regarding the intent, expectations, and feedback from individuals and teams is necessary.[238] Developing communication skills requires intentional effort. Leaders need discernment and perception in communication since there are times when followers do not communicate clearly.[239] Emotional intelligence and cultural awareness help the leader read between the lines and understand what the individual is expressing through non-verbal clues or what they are not saying.[240] An emotionally intelligent leader shares and responds to emotions, communicates action, and channels emotions to meet objectives.[241] Moreover, Johnson and Hackman state that influential leaders successfully integrate emotion and cognition while overcoming physical and mental fatigue, managing stress, and resisting group pressures.[242]

Leaders who have emotional intelligence are self-aware. They know how they will react and respond emotionally in various situations.[243] Emotionally intelligent leaders can also perceive and respond

---

[236] Baldoni 2003.
[237] Ibid.
[238] Karuvelil 2015.
[239] Karuvelil 2015.
[240] Momeny and Gourgues 2019.
[241] Johnson and Hackman 2018.
[242] Ibid.
[243] Kernis 2003.

to emotions in others. They are in a position of connection with individuals to inspire and motivate them to higher performance levels.[244] Emotionally intelligent leaders also understand interactions between team members and groups. Understanding group dynamics enables the leader to encourage and motivate the whole group.[245] In addition, the leader maintains awareness of the communications between group members that could impact productivity.[246] Influential leaders combine these skills to create an environment of trust and motivation toward higher productivity.

Consider the way Jesus communicated to His disciples. He used parables for instruction that shared emotional intelligence, discernment, and teaching relevant to the culture and period.[247] The parables have multiple layers of meaning and purpose that require His followers to listen and think about what He said and its meaning.[248] In Mark 4 (NASB), Jesus tells the parables of the Sower and Soils to the gathered crowd. He was in a position of connection to the culture and what would grasp the crowd's attention.[249] He also knew that not everyone in the crowd would follow Him or ask questions for deeper meaning. In Mark 4:10, Jesus began teaching His followers and disciples that there will be people who see and hear but do not perceive and understand.[250] The same holds for leaders today. Leaders need cultural awareness and emotional intelligence to meet the understanding of individuals, teams, and organizations.

One of the nuances of emotional intelligence and cultural awareness is flexibility. Leaders must listen, perceive, discern, guide, and react.[251] These actions are intentional and require a great deal of flexibility. Leaders with flexibility can adjust and move as needed, which is necessary for building teams, reacting to problems, and working

---

[244] Grosjean, Resick, Dickson, and Smith 2004.

[245] Johnson and Hackman 2018.

[246] Ibid.

[247] Van Eck 2014.

[248] Viljoen 2019.

[249] Ibid.

[250] Van Eck 2014.

[251] Momeny and Gourgues 2019.

toward goals.[252] Communication also requires flexibility since not every person hears or understands the same way. Jesus alluded to this in Mark 4:12. He explained the parable to His disciples because He knew they would continue teaching and training new believers after He was gone. Influential leaders in a position of connection will use communication, emotional intelligence, and cultural awareness to teach and train.

Cultural awareness

As more organizations move to global operations and locations, communication across cultures is a skill that is necessary to establish and grow a relationship between the parent organization and the new branch. Before a global expansion, a training plan and cultural education benefit the organization.[253] Communication is a critical factor in global leadership development. Cseh, Davis, and Khilji suggest that a global mindset is a learned skill leadership needs for cross-cultural interactions.[254] Training requires communication, particularly in cross-cultural training and developing a global perspective. Developing a global mindset involves communication between the individual and the organization to encourage a commonality that brings cohesiveness.[255] A global perspective also involves individual and collective cultural training in preparation for a position of connection.

Cultural awareness is a vital skill in a global organization. Cultural awareness includes curiosity, mindfulness, flexibility, and thinking differently. Global leaders know from daily work, life experience, and formal training.[256] These components are part of learning cultural awareness. However, leaders must take this further and know how to communicate their knowledge and understanding to their organization. Communication occurs on multiple levels within an

---

[252] Ibid.
[253] Kyvik 2018.
[254] Cseh, Davis, and Khilji 2013.
[255] Felício, Meidutė, and Kyvik 2016.
[256] Cseh, Davis, and Khilji's 2013.

organization and involves equipping individuals with the skills needed for success.[257] Individuals need communication skills to interact with others, build teams, and develop leadership skills.[258] Communication skills are part of the position of connection that organizations need to support cultural awareness and global expansion.

Creativity and innovation

Leaders in a position of connection release intelligence, creativity, and initiative or self-worth in those they serve.[259] Inspirational motivation is a position of connection between leader and follower that moves followers toward performance outcomes that exceed expectations and develops leadership potential.[260] Employee-driven innovation builds community by integrating efforts to implement feasible and reasonable results.[261] Employees are points of connection where ideas and solutions multiply with discussion and commiseration.

Creativity is not natural but cultivated through creative thinking and problem-solving that encourage intelligent thoughts and innovative ideas.[262] A leader's point of connection role in follower creativity is evident in areas such as relational development, organizational climate, and job characteristics. Organizations that support and promote creativity in all employees build trust and commitment, leading to growth strategies.[263] In addition, certain leadership styles encourage creativity and lead to effective teams that produce desirable outcomes at multiple levels.[264]

Howard Schultz, of Starbucks fame, recognized the need for creative intelligence at Starbucks when he hired Wright Massey as

---

[257] Momeny and Gourgues 2019.
[258] Kouzes and Posner 2017.
[259] Winston and Patterson 2006.
[260] Sosik and Jung 2018.
[261] Flocco et al. 2022.
[262] Engstrom 1976.
[263] Sosik and Jung 2018.
[264] Northouse 2019, Sosik and Jung 2018.

vice president of design.[265] Massey's skill in creativity and strategic planning led the design team to develop a comprehensive store design that exceeded Schultz's expectations.[266] Schultz displayed authentic leadership traits by remaining true to his vision of Starbucks while allowing his creative team to present new designs for Starbucks stores. As a point of connection, Schultz enthusiastically encouraged his employees to present creative ideas and solve problems.[267] In addition, Schultz set clear goals and guidance that aligned with his vision that influenced the creative activity of his design team.[268] Leaders like Schultz can impact their employees' creativity through an organizational culture that invites and encourages creative ideas and innovative solutions.

Moreover, leaders offer training in creative problem-solving or content-based skills that further creative development.[269] A leader encouraging ingenuity among all levels of employees generates a point of connection that shows followers that their contributions are essential to organizational success.[270] In addition, communication and listening as necessary and vital components of creativity.[271] If Schultz had not been open to communication and listening to suggestions from Massey and the design team, Starbucks might not have been successful in its creative designs. Successful organizational creativity and innovation come from the point of connection between leader and follower that motivates and inspires excellent ideas.

Leading from the inside out as part of inspirational motivation stirs followers to exceed performance expectations and develop leadership potential.[272] As an effective leader and point of connection, you can help followers achieve more than they thought possible, contributing to team cohesion and achievement. In addition, leaders

---

265 Schultz 1997.
266 Ibid.
267 Semedo, Coelho, and Ribeiro 2016.
268 Shalley and Gilson 2004.
269 Ibid.
270 Engstrom 1976, Northouse 2019.
271 Kouzes and Posner 2017.
272 Sosik and Jung 2018.

who share a vision of the future that is compelling and intriguing encourage followers to explore possibilities and design innovative solutions.[273] Positive emotions and a sense of accomplishment boost a leader's creative behavior, further enhancing the point of connection between leader and follower while working together to shape the future.[274]

Mentor or coach

Leadership capacity expands when mentoring and developing others with a position of connection. Servant leadership is an action of kindness and spirituality from a heart of service to others.[275] Authentic leadership exemplifies honesty, trust, and goodness as a position of connection.[276] People look for authentic, strong leaders in times of trouble. Those who demonstrate strength give people a point of connection for leadership and guidance in times of crisis. Leadership, defined by Northouse, is a process of influence to achieve a common goal.[277] At times, a coach can be a position of connection that helps build and strengthen a leader's ability and skill to influence others.

A coach can inspire others to be a more excellent version of themselves by encouraging self-determination and competence.[278] Leadership as an action process can be developed and learned.[279] Leadership development and coaching encourage and promote leaders to the best of their ability and enhance the organization. An organization that uses coaching enables leaders to elevate their skills and abilities. Corporate culture centers on the organization's core values and beliefs.[280] Employees benefit from a corporate culture strength-

---

[273] Kouzes and Posner 2017.
[274] Lan, Xia, and Yang 2021.
[275] Bell and Habel 2010.
[276] Northouse 2019.
[277] Ibid.
[278] Kouzes and Posner 2017.
[279] Collins 2009, Northouse 2019.
[280] Schein and Schein 2016.

ened with its core values and beliefs.[281] Coaching involves specific planning and coordination tailored to the individual while aligning with corporate values.[282] Individuals in executive positions or transitioning to executive positions require detailed plans and lessons based on their career path.[283] The strategies and lessons should align with the organization's larger goals, the individual's abilities, and career path.[284]

Coaching also requires a long-term commitment by the organization and the individual to realize a substantial transformation of both.[285] Lasting change that affects all levels of an organization has specific characteristics ensuring the success of the individual and the organization. It meets the needs of the individuals and organization; it is long-term; it lays a foundation extending beyond the coaching lessons and the value evolves beyond the individual.[286] One of the rules for leadership is to become the best version of yourself.[287] This principle also applies when mentoring others through character development, role modeling, perspective, and coaching.[288] When leaders invest time in coaching, they become the best version of themselves.

Coaching capabilities are transactional or transformational.[289] Transactional coaching involves specific tactical actions that do not provide long-lasting effects.[290] However, transformational coaching involves individuals and organizations, encouraging a more profound commitment and change.[291] Benefits from transformational coaching include team building, relationship enhancement, and leadership skills that build rapport and boost creativity. Coaching involves high-

---

[281] Collins 2009.

[282] Hunt 2007.

[283] Ibid.

[284] Ibid.

[285] Ibid.

[286] Anderson 2005.

[287] Sosik and Jung 2018.

[288] Ibid.

[289] Anderson 2005.

[290] Ibid.

[291] Ibid.

lighting individual strengths to set and meet goals, improve relationships, and grow as a leader.

Moreover, the benefits of coaching include more motivation, confidence, resourcefulness, and individual value.[292] The organization benefits because employees are valued, which increases their loyalty. Additionally, organizations today have a global footprint. Coaching individuals based on strengths and values show a commitment and dedication to employees by encouraging self-development of their best qualities. In return, the organization becomes more substantial as its employees become stronger and more confident. Coaching also addresses targeted areas for effective management development. In a 2002 study in the United Kingdom, Suzy Wales describes coaching through an "internal and external model of development."[293]

Coaching is not a "one size fits all" for organizations. When adequately leveraged and encouraged among all employees, it is a development tool that creates value for individuals and the organization.[294] Coaches tap into strengths, talents, and personalities, enhancing individual skills and benefiting the organization. Strength assessments are great tools for leaders personally and for followers. Impactful leaders will get to know their followers through strengths assessments, conversations, and work results. Appreciating skills, strengths, and talents helps leaders understand how followers will best engage in the organization. As a point of connection, coaching becomes a valuable investment in personal and professional leadership development.

Social media

"Leaders have an ethical responsibility to attend to the needs and concerns of followers."[295] The organization's credibility relies heavily on the actions and behaviors of the leader. When leaders are in a position of connection, especially in a high-profile position, their

---

[292] Starr 2004.

[293] Wales 2002.

[294] Anderson and Anderson 2011.

[295] Northouse 2019.

actions and words are visible to everyone. Social media is an example of a position of connection where influencers develop content for various subjects, ranging from lifestyle to motherhood, photography, and sports. Influencers' connection with their consumers is an exciting phenomenon perpetuated by likes, "going viral," and number of followers. Social media can promote a positive image, help achieve objectives, and add value to the organization.[296] Categories of social media types include broadcast, dialogue, collaboration, knowledge management, and sociability.[297]

Leaders can incorporate these positions of connection within their organization to disseminate information, influence, encourage, and build relationships. Social media as a means of connection is no longer "trendy or a fad" but rather a primary influencer on how people discern meaning and build identity.[298] Personal or identity branding is commonplace, providing users ample opportunities for self-promotion.[299] Communication via social media is a position of connection that positively and negatively influences others.

Social media outside of organizations can connect people across geographical and cultural boundaries, shared interests, and communities and provide support, promotion, and sharing of ideas and opinions.[300] The impact of social media is seen from the number of users and continuous usage across platforms such as Twitter, Instagram, Facebook, and LinkedIn. Using social media to broadcast does little to encourage dialogue or build relationships. However, through discussion and collaboration, leaders can use social media to connect and build relationships among colleagues, followers, and the community and to reflect on the why and for whom.[301] Discourse and diversity of thought leading to innovation and creativity can bring about positive changes and progress. Tomkins also cautions about the negative side of social media, cyberbullying, and trolling,

---

[296] Paus 2013.
[297] Schlagwein and Hu 2017.
[298] Stoller 2013.
[299] Ibid.
[300] Ibid.
[301] Tomkins 2020.

which is why morals, ethics, and values are vital to the position of connection.[302]

It is incredible how social media platforms have taken over much of our communication. It is not easy to imagine when Facebook and Twitter did not exist. In schools, for example, the online platform is integrated into student affairs, furthering online educational development.[303] For students, integrating social media with education is a natural fit. The professional platform integrated social media as well. Social media is a means of expression, business growth, interaction, and education. In these regards, social media is a valuable communication tool as a position of connection.

However, users must ensure a balance between online presence and face-to-face interactions. There also needs to be ethics involved in the use of social media. Many individuals experience shaming, bullying, or unethical treatment through social media. There is a real danger of addiction to social media in which the user looks for validation through comments or likes and can be devastated when harassed or bullied.

Critical thinking skills are also crucial in using social media. Critical thinking helps process information and discern the validity of the information on social media. Critical thinking skills help individuals determine what good productive content is and what is destructive or harmful. Leaders especially need to be aware of social media and how to incorporate it positively into their message or professional life. A leader's self-awareness and emotional intelligence should not hinge on social media. However, it can be a valuable tool as a position of connection for communication between leader and follower. Leaders who develop their online social media presence must maintain self-awareness and professional and ethical behavior, just as they do in person.

---

[302] Ibid.
[303] Stoller 2013.

Leadership strengths

Leadership is complex, with many theories on what to do and what not to do. Lewis speaks of a moral law that is innate in all humans that internal knowledge between right and wrong contributes to the virtues and vices of leaders.[304] When leaders do what is right, care for their followers, and build up the leaders behind them, they implement their leadership virtues.[305] Moral leadership encourages followers to do their best and aspire to do and be more.

Contrast this with a leader who operates out of vices. A leader who is always out for him or herself, looking for their next big promotion, doing whatever it takes to get ahead, putting self above everyone else. This is called hubristic pride, a vice a leader can have.[306] While these leaders may get promoted and placed in areas of greater responsibility, they will find that people will not work for them. The expression "people do not leave jobs; they leave managers" puts this into words exactly. These types of leaders are often arrogant and prideful and so insecure in their leadership ability and position that they constantly remind people they are the boss.

Leaders who desire to solve problems are beneficial to society and humanity. Leaders who focus on practical outcomes are responsible leaders. In addition, leaders with clear goals can use problem-solving skills to meet goals. Problem-solving skills include defining the problem, gathering information, bringing new understanding to the problem, and designing solutions to solve problems.[307] A leader also needs social judgment skills to keep the problems and solutions in perspective, with both individual and organizational views in mind.[308] Both perspectives help the leader shape the solutions that benefit as many as possible. Social commitment encourages leaders and followers to solve global problems with combined skills and abilities for the most benefit.

---

[304] Lewis 1952.

[305] Sousa and Van Dierendonck 2015.

[306] Yeung and Shen 2019.

[307] Northouse 2019.

[308] Ibid.

A study from Namibia illustrated an example of the social commitment of leadership. The Shack Dwellers Federation of Namibia (SDFN) comprised over six hundred neighborhood-based savings groups that joined together to build housing and infrastructure for the extremely poor.[309] The majority of SDFNs are impoverished women with children. The women leaders of this organization show organizational, communication, listening, and problem-solving skills and reveal a drive to encourage and empower other women to improve their quality of life.[310] The results show transformational leadership enhancing the quality of life for communities in Namibia through the women's position of connection.

Although the results are positive, the question remains whether the sustainability of continued improvement in the SDFN is possible. Any organization that looks to transform, empower, and solve problems needs strong leadership. Leadership and followership are real solutions to societal problem-solving.[311] Leaders and followers are needed in the dynamic actions of communities and societies to identify problems, suggest solutions, and make changes that solve problems. Communities need to recognize good leaders as positions of connection as vital for growth and community progress.

Biblical connections

Leadership as a position of connection is an intriguing way of seeing biblical leadership. Jesus modeled servant leadership and placed the needs of followers above His own. Four servant-leadership traits include empowering followers, stewardship, authenticity, and providing direction.[312] Jesus showed each trait through interactions with His disciples and with compassionate love for humanity. Wisdom through servant leadership demonstrates foresight, intuitiveness, stewardship, and service to others.[313] In addition, servant

---

[309] Barnes, Cowser, and Gutierrez 2017.
[310] Ibid.
[311] Pietraszewski 2020.
[312] Van Dierendonck and Patterson 2015.
[313] Ibid.

leaders design solutions based on moral and virtuous strengths.[314] Leadership strengths, combined with servant leadership, become a position of connection to serve others.

Servant leadership also demonstrates ethical leadership. Principles of ethical leadership include respecting others, serving others, showing justice, manifesting honesty, and building community.[315] Honesty shows a deep appreciation for and confidence in the biblical values by which to live and work. Servant leadership, biblical values, and love for others demonstrate qualities that connect to others with respect and honesty.

Furthermore, servant leadership driven by virtues or deeply held values is foundational in the soul.[316] Servant leaders in a position of connection give followers a vision for themselves, their organization, and the community.[317] Paul also demonstrated these traits throughout his writings in the New Testament. Paul maintained his position of connection with believers through letters and instructions. In Colossians 1:9–12(NASB), Paul told the believers in Colossae that they are always in his prayers for wisdom and strength. He encouraged them to walk in a manner worthy of the Lord. Paul's compassionate love shines through in his description of Jesus and how he rejoices to see the Colossians have good discipline and stability of faith in Christ (Colossians 2:5 NASB). He provides them direction and guidance in maintaining faith in Christ and not allowing worldly philosophy and empty deception to deceive them.

Paul was also interested in transforming lives through the knowledge and understanding of Jesus's death and resurrection. Dynamic growth occurs when leadership encourages transformation.[318] Transformation also occurs when the leader shares the vision with followers and works with followers to fulfill that vision. During Paul's lifetime, he witnessed a change in culture through his influence. Through Paul's love of Christ, we can learn to empower fol-

---

[314] Ibid.

[315] Northouse 2019.

[316] Crowther 2021.

[317] Ibid.

[318] Cooper 2005.

lowers, steward our relationships wisely, be authentic, and provide direction to those who follow.

Christian leaders are to walk in a manner worthy of the calling with humility, grace, tolerance, and love, diligently preserving the unity of the Spirit in the bond of peace (Ephesians 4:1–3 NASB). Without God guiding and equipping us, we would walk as the world and try to accomplish things independently. Providing direction and addressing challenges apply to all leaders and are visible in various biblical leaders.[319] When King David encountered Goliath, he knew God was with him and did not falter. He showed the people how to meet the challenge directly with God. His confidence and courage gave direction and inspiration to Israel so they could defeat the Philistines (1 Samuel 17). When we approach challenges in the same way, we show our followers that overcoming a challenge or difficulty is possible despite evidence to the contrary, but only when we maintain our relationship with the Lord.

Our relationship with God is also what transforms us as leaders. Christian leaders need leadership education that transforms much like grace through faith transforms believers.[320] Christian leaders need biblical examples for education, inspiration, and transformation in their leadership abilities. Leadership training varies from leader to leader and with individual positions and experiences.[321] The result of any training should be a transformation of the leader. Paul and Peter's transformation and leadership show how the transformation looks. The question is how to develop transformational leadership principles into practical training that transforms Christian leaders today. Understanding a position of connection with others through Jesus brings about transformation through knowing who you are and how your leadership can influence others for good.

---

[319] Northouse 2019.
[320] Momeny and Gourgues 2019.
[321] Ibid.

Position of Connection

Who you are

Your position is not dependent on a company, a business, or a station in life. It has nothing to do with your talents, skills, or education. Your position is who you are in your relationship with others. Your position of connection is your relationship with others. It could be as a leader or follower, friend, or acquaintance.

As a Christian, your position of connection is a follower of Jesus. You are in Christ, seated with Him, a child of God, an image bearer of Christ, a light bearer.

What you have

What you have in your position of connection is a relationship with others. As a leader, you have followers; an employee has coworkers; a coach has clients. As a parent, you have children, and so on. Connections or relationships are what you have for encouragement, companionship, love, or a shoulder to cry on. Some relationships last a lifetime, and some are brief. What you gain from each other is what you have, making the position of connection rich and unique.

Your position of connection with God is your relationship through Jesus. As a believer in Jesus, you are seated with Him in the heavens. Christ is your position of connection. You have authority in Christ and bring heaven to earth through your position in Him. You have God-given gifts, talents, and abilities to use for the good of others and to glorify God.

How to walk in it

Your actions, attitude, and values position you to influence others in positive, uplifting ways. Your position of connection is where you interact with your spouse and children, coworkers, friends, family, business associates, and anyone whose life you can affect no matter how brief the connection is. God positions us and sets us up to carry out His plan and purpose on earth. He sent Jesus, and His position is Savior and Redeemer. When we walk in our position of connection with Jesus, we carry out his purposes in love.

Scriptures

> Fear and intimidation are traps that hold you back. However, when you place your confidence in the Lord, you will be seated in the high place. (Proverbs 29:25 TPT)

> He raised us up with Christ the exalted One, and we ascended with him into the glorious perfection and authority of the heavenly realm, for we are now co-seated as one with Christ. (Ephesians 2:6 TPT)

> Good leadership is built on love and truth, for kindness and integrity are what keep leaders in their position of trust. (Proverbs 20:28 TPT)

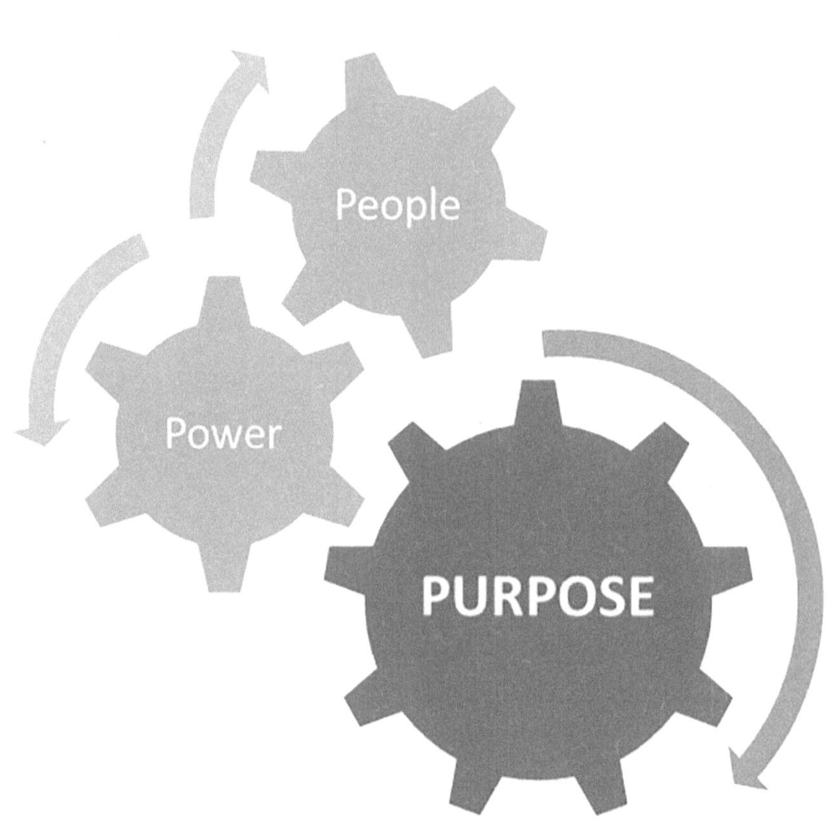

People
Power
PURPOSE

Purpose of Connection

We have a God-given purpose for existence. We have gifts, talents, and abilities to fulfill that purpose. The purpose of connection or meaning for the connection comes from exchanging ideas or providing guidance or a shoulder to lean on. The purpose of connection is, at times, directly understandable and relatable. At other times, the revelation of the purpose of connection happens later. It may be a chance meeting when you gain a piece of information that becomes relevant later. You may provide someone with guidance that helps them discover something new about themselves, or they may do the same for you.

The purpose of connection is not to use or abuse someone or take advantage of them or the information shared. The purpose of connection also may require some trust or vulnerability that opens and expands a relationship, as in mentorship or coaching. Ideally, the purpose of connection points to a specific reason for the relationship. It has substance and depth that goes beyond acquaintance.

Mentoring is also a great way of encouraging organizational or personal growth opportunities. A mentorship culture is about coaching others, assessing their performance, and providing feedback to mentees.[322] Mentoring can also offer a cultural change to the organization that expands the leader's view from technical and political aspects to people. Leaders can create cultural change by assessing a

---

[322] Kouzes and Posner 2017.

problem, how the existing culture contributes to the problem, and developing ways to evolve the culture toward solutions.[323] "Leadership is all about making a positive change."[324] Innovative solutions, cultural change, and growth depend greatly on leadership to connect with employees and improve an organization.

Some relationships like family, close friends, and coworkers have an identifiable purpose. A parent to a child, for example, a supervisor and employee, or a counselor to a client have intentional meaning, with multiple reasons for the connection. Some connections need examining for the purpose, or development continues over time. It is only after reflection that the purpose of connection and its meaning for significance are revealed.

As a soldier, changing units is part of the military experience. However, I always looked for a deeper purpose of connection or meaning and intentionally developed relationships with my fellow soldiers. One significant purpose of connection is suicide prevention. According to the Department of Defense's CY 2021 "Annual Report on Suicide in the Military," the average number of suicides per one hundred thousand soldiers was twenty-three. The statistics do not fully capture the ripple effects suicide or attempted suicide has on multiple soldiers within the unit. I worked with a soldier for two years before he committed suicide. Today, I still question the purpose of that connection and why God allowed it to happen. As much as I talked and shared with that soldier, I could do nothing to help prevent his suicide. The ripple effects lessened, particularly when I helped prevent another soldier from committing suicide. I am grateful that I could help my soldier turn his life around for good, but the emotional impact of suicide remains today.

Purpose and transformation

Purpose gives life meaning. The purpose of connection is when you can impact someone's life for good, help turn their life into a

---

[323] Schein and Schein 2016.
[324] Sosik and Dongil 2015.

good thing, or remind them how important or loved they are. For Christians, the utmost purpose of connection is Jesus. He is the way, the truth, and the life (John 14:6 NASB). As Christians, our very commission is to tell the world about the Savior and to share the good news of great joy. Jesus gives our lives purpose and meaning. He brings everything into sharp focus and reminds us that our lives through Him can provide others with the hope and peace that passes all understanding. When we encounter someone, our purpose of connection is quite evident when Jesus is the center of our life.

Christian leaders should act and behave as one transformed by the gospel. The Christian leader needs self-awareness, intimate knowledge of and expression of morality and ethics based on Scripture. A Christian leader displays values through attitudes and work habits.[325] In the Sermon on the Mount, Jesus describes ethical ideals that seem overwhelming and impossible for humans to attain.[326] However, Jesus also offers practical applications for our transformation. Jesus tells us to love our enemies and pray for those persecuting us (Matthew 5:44 NASB). Prayer for persecutors changes one's thoughts and heart toward forgiveness. As Christian leaders apply the principles Jesus taught, they develop kingdom virtues and engage in the kingdom of heaven on earth.[327] Christian leadership and the application of ethics are a perpetual action of transformation.

Leaders are responsible for the tone, vision, and behavior of those within the organization.[328] When the leader models appropriate ethical behavior, it is an example for others to emulate.[329] A leader's purpose in connecting with others is to help reinforce ethical behaviors for both sides of the relationship and encourage accountability.[330] Jesus's teaching in the Sermon on the Mount is countercultural because it focuses on the core values of love, peace, forgiveness, humility, kindness, and integrity rather than the egotistical and

---

[325] Engstrom 1996.
[326] Fedler 2006.
[327] Ibid.
[328] Ciulla 2014.
[329] Ibid.
[330] Avolio et al.

materialistic values of the world.[331] When problems become evident, leaders must be willing to interrupt unethical behavior.[332] A leader's willingness to confront contrary behavior or actions requires strength and confidence.[333] Ethical behavior requires a transformation from the inside out, as Jesus presented in the Sermon on the Mount (Matthew 5–7) and the Sermon on the Plain (Luke 6:20–49).

The development of leaders requires competency plus vision and a foundation of ethics and morality to raise the level of leadership within an organization. Leaders set the tone for organizational behavior and goals.[334] One of the organizational goals should be ethical behaviors that create an ethical culture that encourages everyone to make ethics a conscious part of their leadership practices. Leadership ethics include the leader's moral character, the ethical legitimacy of the embedded values in the leaders' vision, articulation, and program, and the morality of the leaders' and followers' choices and actions.[335] Leaders need to raise their followers' skill levels, including ethics.[336] Raising the skill level of followers is a kind of empowerment. Authentic empowerment includes moral understanding, commitment, and honesty.[337] Jesus empowered His disciples through teaching, training, and correcting when needed.

Do the right thing

Ethical issues in an organization can also be the result of the culture. Organizational leadership that allows unethical behaviors and practices creates a culture that decreases morale and increases the chances of illegal behavior. Ethical leaders develop and share a common vision or common goal that benefits leaders and followers.[338] An

---

[331] Mabey et al. 2017.

[332] Peters et al. 2017.

[333] Engstrom 1996.

[334] Brown and Mitchell 2010.

[335] Bass and Steidlmeier 1999.

[336] Engstrom 1996.

[337] Ciulla 2014.

[338] Northhouse 2019.

ethical leader also considers the individual's purposes, the community's needs, and the culture.[339] These considerations show authentic transformational leadership that exemplifies ethics and demonstrates how to transform the organizational culture. Ethics is a "communal, collective enterprise, not a solitary one," which underscores the need for a common goal for leaders and followers to achieve together, helping to reinforce the purpose of connection.[340]

Leaders also need to practice ethical behaviors consistently. While every situation a leader faces is different, each requires a foundation of ethics that is determined beforehand. Situational leadership differs by adapting to the situation's needs, either task oriented or relationship oriented.[341] Consistency of ethics helps the leader make moral and right decisions based on the foundation of ethics, which helps in any situation.

Engstrom's guidelines for excellent leadership include honesty and integrity. Subordinates can see through a leader who makes decisions that are not honest or are without integrity.[342] When a leader violates ethical behavior, they undermine the trust of the individuals, which filters down to the lowest levels.[343] The ethical foundation of the organization relies heavily on ethical leadership from the top leader down, which also encourages a culture of ethics. Personal growth is a lifelong process evident in decision-making and leadership-skills development. In Matthew 5–7, Jesus taught how people should be from the inside out. His guidance directed how people live and act from internal thoughts, actions, and decisions that affect others. However, He began by teaching us to seek the kingdom of God first, then we could begin to fulfill His teachings. Ethics is a matter of the heart.[344] Leaders need to ensure their heart is right with God and right with people.

---

[339] Ibid.

[340] Ciulla 2014.

[341] Hersey and Blanchard 1993.

[342] Engstrom 1978.

[343] Ibid.

[344] Ciulla 2014.

Ethics is what flows out from a right heart with God. When we have a foundation that proceeds from the heart of God, there is no doubt that leaders will make ethical choices and decisions. Worldly thoughts and influences can sway a person to make unethical choices. Leaders also need to consider the consequences of their decisions and their effect on the people.[345] The question of motive in those decisions is a consideration when determining the ethicality of a decision or action. Some leaders justify the ends through the means, even when they are unethical, because it seems to achieve positive results.[346]

When an ethical problem arises, leaders need to address the issue with integrity and honesty. Just as bad news does not get better over time, bad behavior does not get better over time. It continues and influences others to behave unethically, especially if the leaders allow it to continue or perform the actions themselves.[347] Christian leaders—any leader—are an example to the organization and the watching world. Jesus said in Matthew 7:26 (NASB), "Therefore everyone who hears these words of Mine and acts on them may be compared to a wise man who builds his house on a rock." Jesus taught a foundation of morals and values and their practical application—for example, judging others by your standards, as in Matthew 7:1. The practical application of this verse reminds a leader to compare their ethical foundation to Scripture rather than man's example. Although Jesus defines many aspects of ethics throughout Matthew 5–7 and Luke 6:20–49, developing ethical behaviors and moral choices takes a lifetime of internal reflection, refinement, and feedback from godly counsel for accountability.

Leadership strategy within an organization is a learning process that involves discernment, discovery, and changes that propel the organization to achieve desired goals and meet or exceed long-term performance potential.[348] The leaders set the organization's mission, values, and vision to describe to others who the organization

---

[345] Bass and Steidlmeier 1999.
[346] Ibid.
[347] Zeni et al. 2016.
[348] Hughes et al. 2013.

is, what they believe in, and their purpose. It is the organization's identity. Strategic leaders assess the internal and external environment as the organization experiences change, gains new information, and grows.[349]

Purposeful culture

An organization must have values, purpose, goals, and objectives that align and complement each other. Business and leadership strategies built on purposeful connection provide direction and guidance at every level and create an organizational culture.[350] Strategic leaders examine the internal and external environments for impacts on performance and culture. Environmental issues such as unchangeable structure, government regulations, and limits of personnel and finance can impact strategy with constraints or directional changes.

A strategic leader is, in a sense, a prophet who can examine the constraints, trends, or directional changes with foresight and help guide the organization into positive and productive courses of action.[351] Authentic present-day prophets' work faces the difficulties the changing world inevitably presents.[352] An organizational strategy that aligns with a system of multiple and interlinking goals is more effective than a single goal.[353] A goal system with strategic planning relates different departmental, organizational, and personal goals to build community, identity, and organizational commitment.[354] In 1 Corinthians 12:14–26, Paul speaks of the members of the body of Christ, and all are a necessary part, uplifting and complimenting each other, acknowledging differences, while uniting under a common purpose of connection to serve others.

---

[349] Ibid.

[350] Schein and Schein 2016.

[351] Beerel 1997.

[352] Ibid.

[353] Ackermann and Eden 2011.

[354] Ibid.

Strategic leadership is the *head* dimension of servant leadership, and operational leadership is the *hands* of servant leadership.[355] Both dimensions of servant leadership come from the *heart*.[356] Aligning goals, vision, mission, and objectives with servant leadership through strategy and operations can create more excellent value for the organization and its people.[357] Servant leadership can also influence the organization's culture and community, leading to meaning in their work and workplace experiences.[358]

A common purpose or shared vision encourages others to realize the dream.[359] There is no common starting place in strategy development without a shared vision, leading to conflict.[360] Jesus taught with a vision of the kingdom of heaven and constantly reminded His disciples of the vision and that the only way to heaven was the belief in Him (John 3:16–17). Jesus was also a strategic leader and taught with intimate knowledge of the Scriptures and the Father, so His teachings carried weight and depth of meaning, applicable two thousand years from when He spoke them.

Intentionally incorporating servant leadership through strategy and operations can help the organization focus on a higher purpose, vision, or mission that adds value to the organization, its people, and the community.[361] Despite environmental issues—such as permanent structure, government regulations, or personal limits on personnel and finance—a servant leader can help align personal and professional goals, giving employees a greater sense of fulfilling a meaningful purpose.[362] Moreover, the servant leader's point of connection can help followers find the purpose of connection through the relationship.

---

[355] Van Dierendonck and Patterson 2015.

[356] Ibid.

[357] Hitt and Ireland 2002.

[358] Williams et al. 2017.

[359] Kouzes and Posner 2017.

[360] Hughes et al. 2014.

[361] Van Dierendonck and Patterson 2015.

[362] Ibid.

As organizations grow and develop, the goals change, and the mission and purpose may change; however, the core beliefs and values of the organization's foundation will continue to align with the mission and purpose. The disciples of Jesus have an ongoing mission and purpose in sharing the good news of salvation. In Acts 2, Peter preaches the gospel of Jesus, the vision Jesus alluded to before His death and resurrection. The shared vision of the gospel of Jesus is the common vision of believers, which has not changed since His death and resurrection over two thousand years ago. Those with a foundation of meaning and purpose in Jesus can apply this to their organizational foundation, leading toward a greater sense of meaning and purpose.[363]

Communication

Leadership communication aims to convey a message, disseminate information, inspire, and guide. Communication reflects the values of the leader, coupled with the organization's values that express and indicate culture and climate.[364] Leaders know and understand how to get a message out that directly conveys intent and meaning. Examples of types of leadership messages include vision, transformation, call to action, expectation, coaching, and listening.[365] The leadership message gives the pertinent information that provokes the listener to the next idea or action. Good communication should establish a purpose of connection understood by all.

Consider the leadership of Deborah from Judges 4–5 in the Old Testament. Deborah was a prophet who judged Israel when Jabin was the king of Canaan. Deborah's reputation as a prophetess and judge was established and well-known. She called Barak son of Abinoam to her and delivered a message from the Lord to go into battle against Sisera, captain of Jabin's army. Deborah's message, her purpose of connection, was a call to action that was simple and direct. She deliv-

---

[363] Peters, Rocks, and Doval 2017.
[364] Baldoni 2013.
[365] Ibid.

ered a command from the Lord with confidence and boldness, supported by her position as a prophetess of Israel. Barak also requested Deborah to go with him to the battlefield. Here, Deborah demonstrated a willingness to lead by example and to support Barak with her presence and guidance.

Deborah was the expert. Baldoni states that the expert is "the keeper of the mission."[366] Deborah understood the mission given by God and delivered the message directly to Barak (Judges 4:6–7). Barak asked her to accompany him and the soldiers to the battlefield, and she agreed (Judges 4:8–9). Deborah's position of connection as a prophetess, judge, and faithful deliverer of God's Word exemplifies an expert who leads in words and deeds that focus on fulfilling the God-given message.

Another biblical example of the purpose of connection was the relationship between David and Saul. David had an enemy in King Saul. David's leadership grew through the conflict by showing how David had to grow in his leadership skills and communication with the Israelites. Although Samuel anointed David as king as a boy, David grew into his leadership position; he earned it through admirable character, nobility, and generosity.[367] David led by example, communicating to the people of Israel his strength, confidence, and desire to lead them well. The purpose of connection between David and Saul resulted in multiple levels of emotion and confrontational experiences that shaped David's path to kingship.

David exhibited several hallmark leadership qualities that defined him and demonstrated his leadership abilities.[368] These qualities include diplomacy, a foundation in spiritual values, challenging and motivating his followers, and steadfast devotion to seeking the Lord.[369] David constantly communicated to his followers the importance of a relationship with the Lord and dedication to serving Him no matter what (2 Samuel 6:12–15). David set an example of leadership and communication for others to follow.

---

[366] Ibid.

[367] Engstrom 1976.

[368] Ibid.

[369] Ibid.

However, David's leadership and purpose of connection became tarnished when he eliminated Bathsheba's husband and took her as his wife. Communication for leaders is in their words and actions. How they portray themselves and demonstrate internal ethics and values speak volumes. Although David made an error in judgment, the prophet Nathan held him accountable.[370] Leaders need accountability when communicating a message that contradicts morals and values.[371] Leaders need to communicate with clarity and consistency in their words and actions.

Noah was a leader with a God-given purpose of connection and a visionary. A visionary leader is one "whose ardent belief outweighs their words."[372] In Genesis 6:8, Noah found favor in the eyes of the Lord. Genesis 6:9 says Noah walked with God. These two verses describe Noah as one whose values and beliefs aligned with God's. As a visionary, Noah received the word of the Lord and accepted that vision. He walked with God; he knew and understood God's heart. Noah accepted and obeyed God's instructions to build and inhabit the ark without question. Noah needed that relationship with God as a foundation to accept and fulfill the Lord's vision for him and his family.

Leaders are responsible for communicating the organization's vision and the values and beliefs that uphold the vision. The vision should be the pursuit of excellence in serving the Lord, regardless of calling or vocation.[373] Christian leaders must use foresight and insight to establish the vision and look to the future fulfillment of that vision.[374] When Jesus walked the earth, His vision was of humanity and what His death and resurrection would do for humanity (John 14). His foundation was a relationship with God (John 14:10–11). His life, death, and resurrection fulfilled His purpose on earth.

As Noah and Jesus fulfilled the Lord's vision, Christian leaders are responsible for encouraging and guiding in fulfilling the vision.

---

[370] Spielman 1999.

[371] Ibid.

[372] Baldoni 2003.

[373] Engstrom 1976.

[374] Ibid.

A problem-solving skill leaders need is articulating a vision that helps "followers understand, make sense of, and act on the problem."[375] Communication and persuasion skills are essential to sharing and understanding the vision.[376] Leaders who communicate well with followers inspire a shared vision with the imagination of exciting and elevating possibilities.[377] Visionary leaders live from the inside out, with passion and the conviction of possibilities.[378]

Although most leaders have a naturally specific style, leadership communication is not a one-size-fits-all approach. The leader needs to hear and understand followers to develop productive relationships, not in the sense of changing to suit everyone but in developing productive relationships with followers. Your style as a leadership communicator varies with the situation.[379] Leaders need to know their audience, how to connect, and what appeals to the audience. The purpose of the message contributes to the communication style.[380] Since the message varies, the communication style varies as well.

Moses, for example, demonstrated authority when confronting Pharaoh with the Lord's demand to free the Hebrew people. In Exodus 3–4, God established Moses and Aaron as the experts who went before Pharaoh to speak the words God gave to them. They were to speak with the authority and command of the Lord. Moses also instructed the people from the Lord regarding the Law and commandments. He was part of transforming the Hebrews from a slave nation to a nation with laws, government, and guidance from God. Although Moses continually questioned God's choice of him as a leader of the Hebrews, God fulfilled many promises to the Hebrews through the leadership of Moses.

---

[375] Northouse 2019.

[376] Ibid.

[377] Kouzes and Posner 2017.

[378] Baldoni 2003.

[379] Ibid.

[380] Ibid.

Creative purpose

Additionally, leadership involves identifying organizational problems and designing innovative, thoughtful, and productive solutions. Like corporate America, the United States military has a recruiting and retention problem. Recruitment is forty-five thousand below the goal intent, and retention of service members is dropping at an alarming rate. Corporate America recently experienced a "great resignation" following the COVID-19 pandemic, resulting in a considerable loss in the workforce. New enlistment numbers are lower than in previous years, and many currently serving service members elect not to extend their service. Recruitment and retention problems become a more significant issue of force readiness. In addition, the leadership perspective of millennials and Generation Z causes some friction and adds to the retention and recruitment problem.[381] The differences in leadership styles and techniques also require a shift from conformity to adaptability and communication.[382]

Leaders should identify and accept challenges before generating ideas that lead to a solution.[383] Recruiting and retention in the military require commitment and thinking outside the box for solutions pertinent to the new generation of service members. Good and bad leadership affects a service member's decision to reenlist and continue military service.[384] The recruiting and retention problem in the armed forces is multilayered and requires multiple levels of insight and commitment to developing strategic solutions. A leader identifies the problem and works with others toward an impactful solution by sharing knowledge and information.[385] Soldiers receive training to understand the purpose of connection through military tactics and strategy training in preparation for wars.

The purpose of connections through networking is essential in any organization. In addition, cultural assessment, communication,

---

[381] Hanks 2022.

[382] Miller 2019.

[383] Michalko 2010.

[384] Hanks 2022.

[385] Kouzes and Posner 2017.

and growth opportunities are also areas worth examining that can contribute to an overview of the organization where leaders can assess areas for positive change. In addition, the vision and mission statement of the organization provides employees with the organizational foundation and purpose. Leaders identify problems, drive innovation, and work with others to design positive solutions to impact an organization.[386] A *renovation* approach where leaders examine each *room* of the organization for attributes and problems will help identify areas for improvement or change.[387] Leaders who model collaboration, knowledge, idea sharing, and information exchange contribute to creativity and innovation in problem-solving.[388] This is the leader-member exchange theory, where relationships between leaders and followers are esteemed, and the goals of the leader, follower, and organization are advanced.[389]

Leaders also challenge and develop colleagues so they progress in professional development, and the organization retains the best and brightest.[390] As a new leader, assessing individuals, the organizational culture, and communication needs provide vital information and assistance in identifying problems and designing solutions. Knowledge sharing, internal and external collaboration, and cultivating positive and creative solutions enhance colleague relationships.[391] Every effort to improve the organization reinforces the collaborative efforts to support the vision and mission statement.

Strategic changes without communication from the top down can harm an organization and its employees. Leadership's value on employee engagement and collaboration helps or hinders the solution effort. A crucial element of project strategy is the relationship between projects and strategy execution.[392] The challenges and prob-

---

[386] Ibid.

[387] Mihalko 2006.

[388] Carmeli et al. 2013.

[389] Northouse 2019.

[390] Sosik and Dongil 2018.

[391] Carmeli et al. 2013.

[392] Pedersen and Ritter 2018.

lems come from several areas, including communication, strategic planning, and collaboration on multiple levels.

Strategic alignment and employee engagement through collaboration should provide focus and clarity on solving problems and communication efforts. Mind mapping is a great start and a technique others can use to brainstorm solutions.[393] Collaborating with colleagues through the mapping process should provide creative ideas for multiple challenges, enhancing the organizational culture by adding value to employees' creative innovation. Starting from a common purpose and imagining the possibilities result in actionable solutions using readily available information and resources. Above all, vertical and horizontal communication efforts are critical components of solutions, especially when implementing new products and strategies.

Innovation and creativity in the modern age have grown substantially and affected every aspect of human existence: quantum computing, innovative medicine, virtual reality, and artificial intelligence, to name a few. The question is, have our sense of ethics or ethical guidelines grown with advancing technology, or has pursuing innovation left behind the ethical standards that guided us for thousands of years?

The role of ethics in innovation cannot be understated. Ethics is the values and morals an individual or society finds appropriate or desirable. Ethics involves personal values, morals, and virtues that guide decisions about right and wrong. Honesty, trust, fairness, and principles are part of an ethical leader's character. Authentic ethical leadership provides a foundation from which a leader operates with vision, integrity, and honesty in serving others. Several conditions that become destructive to innovation without a moral foundation include the following:

- Empty vision: lack of purpose and meaning
- Empty mind: lack of innovation and creativity
- Empty heart: moral relativism without consciousness and care

---

[393] Mihalko 2006.

- Empty spirit: lack of spiritual maturity
- Empty sensitivity: lack of emotional intelligence
- Empty character: unethical, immoral, without integrity[394]

Innovation and creativity from an ethical foundation provide purpose, meaning, and growth within an organization, generating new ideas and creative works. Innovation and creativity need the balance provided by moral standards, not swayed by current culture or feelings. Authentic leadership comes from the heart that is aligned with God's vision and positioned to serve the needs of others. Innovation that comes from God's vision is full of meaning and purpose. A leader's moral character builds a foundation of ethical leadership, the legitimacy of values, and the morality of processes in which the leaders and followers engage. Innovation can work for moral intention and consequences through authentic, ethical leadership rather than egotistical and selfish gains. Research shows that ethical leadership produces positive emotions, including empathy and enthusiasm, that provoke innovation.

Abraham Lincoln said, "If we cultivate the moral world within us as prodigiously as we cultivate the physical world around us, then perhaps we can endure." He spoke these words during a divisive time in American history. However, his words are appropriate as a reflection on innovation and ethics. Leaders who cultivate morals and values will encourage followers to do the same when they develop their physical world through innovation.

Encouraging ingenuity is a way to challenge the current system or invent new products or methods.[395] A leader who shows interest and excitement for innovation creates a culture of creativity and progress within the organization, leaving no room for innovation antibodies. Built-in organizational resilience is a good way for organizations to establish and prepare for innovation change. A resilient organization is stable and a prerequisite for disruption and change.[396]

---

[394] Duignan and Bhindi 1995.
[395] Enstrom 1976.
[396] Anderson et al. 2019.

Moreover, long-term growth comes from innovation, which causes necessary disruption contrary to innovation antibodies. However, the more resilient the organization, the more it responds positively to change.

Positive global leadership is effective across cultures.[397] Positivity is dynamic and can counter the resistance to change, restoring the balance that brings learning and growth.[398] On the contrary, creativity and innovation often lead to challenges to the status quo, resulting in anxiety and uncertainty felt significantly by innovation antibodies or those resistant to change. Leaders with high emotional intelligence recognize the need for stability in organizational structure, processes, creativity, and innovation.[399] These leaders also recognize the importance of assisting those resistant to change.

Innovation antibodies

Organizational resilience can positively impact the balance between preparation for change and the ability to enact change with positive results. Organizational resilience welcomes information gathering, generating, and modifying ideas that encourage creativity and imagining possibilities.[400] Incorporating resilience into the organizational culture can help reduce the resistance to change from innovation antibodies. Schein and Schein suggest reducing learning anxiety with psychological safety.[401] Several factors that create psychological safety include a positive, compelling vision; formal training involving the learner; team building; and positive role models.[402] Supportive elements can help create psychological safety that can counter innovation antibodies.

Because we know that innovation antibodies occur at various organizational levels, leaders can take several steps to promote a cul-

---

[397] Youssef and Luthans 2012.
[398] Ibid.
[399] Zhou and George 2003.
[400] Ibid.
[401] Schein and Schein 2015.
[402] Ibid.

ture of innovation and creativity. Leaders should create a foundation of vision and mission, incorporating innovation and creativity, ensuring all employees know the purpose and meaning of new ideas that encourage progress. In addition, leaders must remind everyone in the organization that creativity and innovation are welcome and encouraged, fostering a culture of employee involvement.

Integrating innovation management with organizational behavior helps implement, maintain, and enhance innovation and creativity. Although innovation antibodies can cause conflict in an organization and derail innovation, leaders can utilize organizational community-building to support initiatives and help alleviate concerns about change.[403] Organizational resilience builds risk awareness, cooperation, agility, and improvisation.[404] Combining resilience with leadership skills and a culture of innovation can help tip the balance toward creation and away from antibodies.

Resistance to change is an emotional process that is necessary for learning.[405] Leaders and managers can incorporate two methods of employee-driven initiatives that can help overcome emotional resistance to change. A community-building approach is open and participative, with ideas and suggestions visible to everyone, encouraging innovation.[406] Another approach is a solutions-based practice with a closed, controlled structure where employees produce and implement innovative solutions.[407] Methods of innovation that build relationships and encourage creative thoughts and ideas could help innovation antibodies overcome emotional resistance and grow through the learning process.

Organizational success depends on creativity, innovation, and change. The environment outside an organization constantly changes. Organizational leaders need to incorporate creativity and innovation within to meet the changes outside of the organization. Leaders who disregard or dismiss creative and innovative ideas protect

---

403 Flocco, Canterino, and Cagliano 2022.
404 Anderson et al. 2019.
405 Block 2011.
406 Flocco, Canterino, and Cagliano 2021.
407 Ibid.

what they know and what works for the organization.[408] Creativity and innovation challenge what is known and imagine future possibilities. Some leaders have difficulty integrating the unknown into their thought processes, discouraging creativity and innovation.[409] However, leaders who enhance the creativity and innovation climate of the organization through clear guidance, support, encouragement, and direction see more success than those that do not.[410]

Creativity, innovation, and change also require discipline and structure. Innovation outcomes measured through return on investment, financial impact, and transparency in spending provide feedback and show tangible success.[411] An intentional and disciplined approach encourages responsibility and wisdom through the creative process and investment of time and resources into innovation. Additionally, structure and discipline encourage ethical practices of creativity and innovation. An ethical environment promotes creative thinking, team building, trust, and employee empowerment.[412] Transformational leaders encourage employees' creative input, adding value to the individual and the organization that helps innovation succeed.

"Did God's innovative creativity stop after creation?" is a fascinating question that involves multiple layers of searching for answers. The Bible is full of continued examples of innovative creativity. God created Adam, His image and likeness, with His creative nature. When God created the earth and all the animals, He gave Adam the task of naming them (Genesis 2:19), meaning he used his imagination to name them. God wants mankind to use imagination to discover Him and seek Him out.

Scripture and personal experience show that God uses innovation to know Him, communicate with Him, and accomplish His will for mankind.[413] Mankind's creativity and innovation come from

---

408 Berkun 2010.
409 Kouzes and Posner 2017.
410 Isaksen and Lauer 2002.
411 Ikeda and Marshall 2016.
412 Ibid.
413 Oster 2009.

the desire to imitate the Creator through gifts, talents, and abilities. Christian innovation derives from envisioning a future possibility, a new perspective, or an expression of beauty that brings knowledge of God to others.[414] God conceals the revelation of His Word in His glory and reveals the honor of kings through their search for the deeper meaning of all God says (Proverbs 25:2 TPT). God encourages us to seek Him through Scripture and a relationship with Him.

Paul alludes to creative innovation in 1 Corinthians 12:17–20. When teaching about spiritual gifts, Paul pointed out the variety of spiritual gifts necessary for the body of Christ. The body of Christ requires the diversity of the spiritual gifts to function correctly, to encourage and edify believers and bring glory to God. "The work of our hands and the example of our being should draw others to God."[415] Paul also points out the relationship between individuals to the body and vice versa. Current research supports individual creativity contributing to organizational innovation and suggests that organizational innovation influences individual creativity.[416] Creativity and innovation are also part of outstanding leadership that advances civilization with vision and imagination.[417] Mankind is creative and innovative because God created us that way to accomplish His will and purpose on earth.

Leadership is of great importance for creativity and innovation to flourish. Leaders who encourage change and productivity develop strategies for productivity and profitability, including creativity and innovation.[418] Authentic leaders can create a culture of creativity and innovation that encourages growth and development.[419] Leadership can "enhance or hinder workplace creativity and innovation."[420]

---

[414] Ibid.
[415] Ibid.
[416] Litchfield, Ford, and Gentry 2015.
[417] Engstrom 1976.
[418] Adair 2007.
[419] Cerne et al. 2013.
[420] Hughes et al. 2018.

Moreover, employees respond with creativity and innovation within a supportive climate and culture enhanced by leaders.[421]

In addition to leadership and culture, individual self-awareness, drive, focus, awareness of strengths and weaknesses, and subject expertise contribute to an individual's creativity and innovation.[422] The combination of individual creativity, culture, and leadership provides an environment conducive to the successful implementation of innovation. Positive future strategy and risk acceptance are two additional conditions enhancing innovation's success. Focused goals, corporate purpose, and future vision help organizations build on past success while creating a path toward a desired future.[423] Leaders are responsible for ensuring employees understand the organization's future vision, provide guidance, and encourage a culture of creativity and innovation. Innovation also involves the acceptance of risk. Creative failures can be costly; however, the lessons learned and growth gained to benefit the individual and the organization can eventually result in innovative successes.[424]

Critical components of creativity and innovation success involve multiple levels of interaction between leader, follower, and organization. The culture of the organization, structured by leadership supporting a creative environment, provides the components for innovation success. Creative innovation raises new questions and possibilities that can lead to positive strategic organizational outcomes. Creativity and innovation are what organizations need to expand and grow beyond their current boundaries. A good way for leaders to nurture and critically develop ideas is through feedback.[425] Good feedback has three goals: terminate worthless ideas and proposals, expose all negative aspects of a viable idea for refinement, and provide constructive suggestions.[426] Thoroughly working through

---

[421] Khalili 2016.

[422] Ghosh 2015.

[423] Adair 2007.

[424] Ibid.

[425] Mihalko 2007.

[426] Ibid.

ideas, plans, or concepts encourages participants to look for flaws or risks that need addressing before implementation.

Leaders and team members can also use strategic foresight techniques to generate creative and innovative ideas. Strategic foresight—or futurist characteristics—include playfulness, analytical questioning, openness to experimentation, delight in telling your story, and openness to giving and receiving criticism.[427] Strategic foresight takes creativity and imagination to see the organization's future without restricting how things look today.[428] Strategic foresight can inspire creativity and innovation within individuals, helping the organization evolve future possibilities for the organization that also values the individual.

Implementation is one of the most important things to remember about creativity and innovation. "When you feel your idea has reached the end, implement it."[429] Too much time refining an idea can make it ineffective or obsolete, resulting in a lost opportunity. Leaders can waste time focusing on perfecting an idea and miss the market or target audience. Incorporating the exploration of the future should be a routine and continuous activity, equally applicable to creativity and innovation.[430] Just as iron sharpens iron, so one man sharpens another (Proverbs 27:17), actively engaging with others through creative thoughts and ideas enhances and builds ideas and strategies for the future.

As a leader, knowing your true self is knowing your purpose of connection. Leaders can be born from learning, growth, and development. By knowing yourself, your strengths and weaknesses, and your purpose, you can learn skills that strengthen your ability to lead others, which creates powerful connections.[431] Leadership is knowing who you are, what you have, and how to walk in it, which is a continuous process. The inner drive is a leader's internal desire to be better

---

[427] Coates 2004.

[428] Marsh, McAllum, and Purcell 2002.

[429] Mihalko 2007.

[430] Coates 2004.

[431] Engstrom 1976.

to lead better.[432] In Hebrews 11 (NASB), Paul writes of leaders and their characteristics for our encouragement and self-development. It takes time, commitment, purpose, and connection to develop your leadership abilities and then to recognize skills and abilities in others to lead them into their destiny.[433]

Purpose of Connection

Who you are

Your purpose of connection is to be prepared when you encounter others. Preparation is establishing your beliefs, morals, and values to be ready to share with others. It is to know how to walk and live with integrity in your actions, developing a good character so your encounters with others are genuine and mutually beneficial. Who you are as an individual, a family member, or a member of an organization helps place you in positions or places that could be divine connections. Preparing for encounters with others helps define and identify the purpose of those connections.

What you have

You have within you a God-given purpose that gives you hope and a future. Your gifts, talents, and abilities, combined with critical thinking and education, provide authenticity and leadership traits that can impact others for good. When you decide who you are and your purpose, you have what you need to engage others positively and help them discover their purpose.

How to walk

The shared purpose of connection increases collaboration, networking, and power that supports the connection. Relationships

---

[432] Ibid.
[433] Ibid.

with others provide a chance to share testimony, unlock doors, and fulfill the purposes God has divinely prepared for you. As you walk with integrity and character, you bring out the best in others.

Scripture

> "For I know the plans that I have for you" declares the Lord, "plans for welfare and not for calamity to give you a future and a hope."
> (Jeremiah 29:11 NASB)

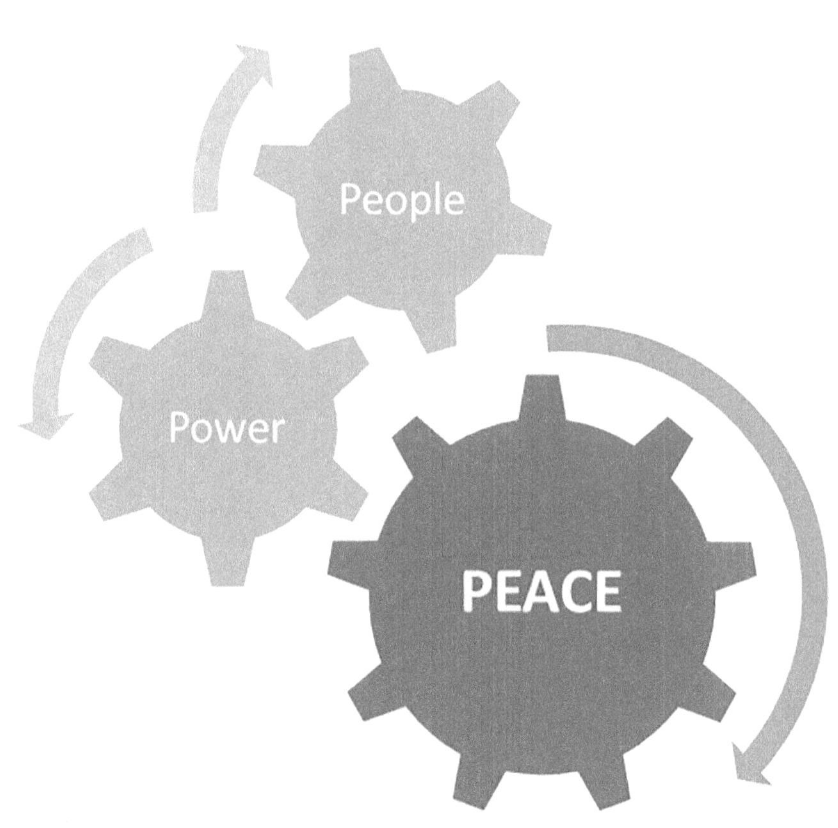
People
Power
PEACE

CHAPTER 5

Peace of Connection

Are you at peace where you are? Consider your connections and the relationships you have with family. Family dynamics and interactions are fluid; most people interact with family daily. Whether caring for young children, parents, or a spouse, there is an ebb and flow between you and your family. At times, it may be chaotic or full of tension. Peace may be elusive at times, but the hope is that there is peace of connection with family.

Take a look at work connections. Is there peace of connection with your coworkers? There are always "sandpaper people" who get under your skin or cause friction that disrupts the peace of connection. Are you at peace with your work? We often stay with an employer because it is comfortable, steady, and a safety net. I recently retired from the military, and when that safety net of employment, income, and comfort zone of work was gone, I felt a sense of loss, a disruption to my peace about the decision to retire. I could see it as a time to panic or jump back into a familiar position and a steady paycheck. However, I had to ask myself if I would be at peace with my decision. Ultimately, I decided on my heart, and with my husband's support, I decided to focus on finishing my doctorate. I am thankful I made that decision, as it came with peace of connection.

Peace of love

In the letter to the Corinthian church, Paul covers various topics. First Corinthians 13, considered the love chapter, expounds on the foundation of love that strengthens the servant-leadership model. Leadership is grounded in love.[434] First Corinthians 13:4–7 lists the actions of love: patience, kindness, forgiving, truth, forbearance, belief, hope, and endurance. The actions of a servant leader support followers with love from the heart. Servant leaders desire to serve others, help them achieve goals, and become more than they thought possible.[435]

Paul also discusses growth and maturity in 1 Corinthians 13:11. Servant leaders impart wisdom and knowledge to followers to assist their intellectual, spiritual, and emotional growth through experience and maturity. As followers grow and mature, their contributions add value to the organization.[436] The followers' learning, growing, and developing process is more valuable to servant leaders than attaining power and position.

The agape love Paul describes is practical for transforming lives, reconciling relationships, and producing good fruit, individually and corporately.[437] Paul reminded the Corinthian church that their actions and decisions influenced believers and unbelievers. Paul's reminder applies to servant leadership today. Servant leaders who teach, train, and mentor with love set aside selfish gain and ambition to help develop followers and influence the next generation of servant leaders.[438] Organizations that recognize and incorporate servant-leadership training help nurture emotional intelligence, ethical decision-making, and empowering skills.[439] Practical application of servant leadership founded on love bears fruit from the individual to the organization and surrounding community.

---

[434] Bell 2014.

[435] Whittington et al. 2005.

[436] Northouse 2019.

[437] Bell 2014.

[438] Crowther 2018.

[439] Northouse 2019.

Peace Through Harmony and Cooperation

Unity and collaboration are essential in leadership. The promotion of unity and collaboration begins with a vision. Leaders challenge others to imagine exciting and ennobling possibilities by sharing a common vision.[440] When Paul speaks of the spiritual gifts in 1 Corinthians 12, he describes the body of Christ as having varieties of gifts but the same Spirit. This Spirit binds Christians in unity and collaboration in the love of Christ. When the church operates in the unity of the Spirit, it achieves more than disagreements over gifts or who is the greatest.

In organizations outside the church, unity and collaboration can be achieved through a shared vision. Servant leaders can help provide the vision of service for the betterment of followers, the organization, and the community. Servant leadership has "unique and positive impacts on subordinates, teams, and organizations."[441] Servant leadership brings a sense of accomplishment, positive emotions, and innovative ideas.[442] Unity and collaboration are sorely needed in the United States of America right now. We have lost the vision of America as a beacon of freedom in Christ, espousing a division of thought, culture, and purpose instead. As servant leaders and Christians, we serve others and build followers for a better future.

Still, we also must stand firm in the Christian principles and ideas from Scripture. We are to be in the world but not of the world. Many people do not know their identity in Jesus and have lost their way. We need to clearly remember Paul's words to the Corinthians that the same God works in and through all things, and we are all members of one body, with one Spirit in Christ Jesus.

Paul had the daunting task of changing the minds and culture of the Corinthian believers. The love of Jesus changed their hearts, and to follow His example of servant leadership, their minds had to renew (Romans 12:2), which would help change the culture, first of

---

[440] Kouzes and Posner 2017.
[441] Lan et al. 2021.
[442] Ibid.

believers and then the rest of the city. The church leaders in Corinth needed to think and act differently than the secular leaders to set an example for others. Paul's letters highlighted areas of needed correction, with much encouragement and solid teaching applicable today.

Servant leadership and peace of connection

Servant leaders must have high moral values and excellence to be effective.[443] It is part of Paul's message to the Corinthians (1 Corinthians 5), where he discussed arrogance, boasting, and immorality. Believers are to hold one another accountable, do what is right, and correct one another as needed. Paul's technique of servant leadership is full-range transformational and transactional leadership with love, encouragement, and corrective demands when necessary.[444]

Contemporary servant leaders must also follow Paul's leadership techniques when leading others. Leaders walking in authenticity and integrity cannot be afraid to correct followers when needed, always with love and encouragement. Authentic servant leaders are not exclusive to the church or any other organization. Servant leaders carry these qualities and live them from the inside out. It is a way of life, built on a foundation of love in Christ Jesus, that servant leaders walk out and demonstrate no matter where they go and whom they encounter. Leadership is a relational process having less to do with position and more with community and relationships God has placed in our path.[445]

Servant leadership as a lifelong process helps define a legacy and trains the next generation of servant leaders. Excellence in Christian leadership is a process that requires constant evaluation, correction, and improvement.[446] The process is what Paul describes in the letters to the Corinthians. In 1 Corinthians 9:24–27, Paul speaks of the process involving self-control, discipline, training, direction, and vision. The servant-leader process also depends on those four cat-

---

[443] Spears 1998.
[444] Whittington et al. 2005.
[445] Bell 2014.
[446] Engstrom 1976.

egories to develop the leader within and then pass that process to followers. Those who develop the four categories within become at peace with who they are and can help others find peace.

As mentors, servant leaders combine organizational-specific training with relationships and follower development.[447] The mentorship process is changing lives to reflect love, care, and concern back to the mentor.[448] When followers become leaders, they, in turn, change lives with the love, care, and concern as they were shown.[449] Mentorship for the servant leader also includes a continuous process of internal improvement. Mentoring followers through self-improvement, goals, foresight, skill building, and community relationships also empowers followers.[450] With empowerment also comes responsibility.

Paul discusses accountability in 2 Corinthians 13:1–3. In this third reminder, he reminds the believers again that sin is not tolerated and that even through weakness, the power of God within enables strength. Paul's example applies to servant leaders and followers for accountability. Servant leaders are accountable for their actions, just as followers are accountable for their actions.[451] Accountability helps build the relationship between leader and follower while encouraging each other to uphold values and morals. Accountability helps leaders and followers maintain excellence throughout the leadership process.[452] As Paul (2 Corinthians 13:10), accountability is for building up and not tearing down.

Servant leadership originated with Robert Greenleaf in the 1970s. Servant leadership places the follower first, empowers them,

---

[447] Pearson 2012.
[448] Whittington et al. 2005.
[449] Ibid.
[450] Murari and Gupta 2012.
[451] Northouse 2019.
[452] Engstrom 1976.

and equips them to develop their full potential.[453] A definition of servant leader is as follows:

> One who selects, equips, trains, and influences one or more followers who have diverse gifts, abilities, and skills and focuses the follower on the organization's mission and objectives, causing the follower to willingly and enthusiastically extend spiritual, emotional and physical energy in a concerted, coordinated effort to achieve the organizational mission and objectives.[454]

Servant leadership is also a paradox in which the leader serves and leads with a unique perspective.[455]

Servant leadership involves relationships with people and acknowledging diversity while achieving common values and goals and maintaining the uniqueness of the follower.[456] A servant leader's primary concern is serving others through demonstrating and teaching values and morals. Servant leaders' actions stem from "What can I do for you?" with a desire to affect growth in the follower, leading to positive outcomes for the organization. Servant leadership's moral basis distinguishes it from transformational leadership. It involves sacrificing one's ego for a higher purpose and commitment to a worthy cause while maintaining ethical and moral values and dependence on relationships.[457] The servant leader places others before self while looking to fulfill a greater purpose than selfish whims and desires.

The servant leader builds trust with followers through actions and behaviors that display moral and ethical values in everything they do and their relationships with people.[458] Leaders within an organization create, build, and maintain trust through their actions,

---

[453] Northouse 2019.

[454] Winston and Patterson 2006.

[455] Northouse 2019.

[456] Winston and Patterson 2006.

[457] Parolini et al. 2009.

[458] Joseph and Winston 2004.

decisions, communication, and interactions with others.[459] Modeling servant leadership affects the organization's trust culture in positive ways.[460] Trust is a crucial element within organizational culture, affecting behavior and interactions between colleagues and leaders.[461] Trusting one another brings peace to a relationship while building solid connections.

Servant leadership also engages people on a different level than other leadership styles. While the primary focus for followers is meeting organizational goals, the leaders serve those working to achieve those goals.[462] It is why relationships are vital to servant leadership. The leader interacts with followers, equips, trains, and influences them to build them up while meeting organizational goals.[463] The outcomes of servant leadership are "follower performance and growth, organizational performance, and societal impact."[464] Servant leaders who engage followers look for the gifts, callings, and abilities and work with the follower to put them to good use for their improvement and to meet organizational goals.[465]

The servant leader understands that the commitment level applies to multiple levels of engagement and interaction, from personal and organizational relationships to communities and audiences outside the organization.[466] Although difficult to measure, the impact of servant leadership is viable and visible in modern organizations, as well as Paul's demonstration of servant leadership in Philippians 2:1–18. Servant leadership incorporates moral and spiritual dimensions needed in modern organizations.[467] Servant leadership requires a commitment by the leader to place themselves in a position of service to others, which takes strong character and conviction.[468]

---

[459] Ibid.

[460] Ibid.

[461] Ibid.

[462] Gandolfi, Stone, and Deno 2017.

[463] Winston and Patterson 2006.

[464] Northouse 2019.

[465] Gandolfi et al. 2017.

[466] Winston and Patterson 2006.

[467] Sendjaya et al. 2008.

[468] Ibid.

An integrative definition of servant-leadership theory based on the Beatitudes in Matthew 5 includes the following:

- Humility
- Concern for others
- Controlled discipline
- Seek what is right and good for the organization
- Show mercy in beliefs and actions with all people
- Focus on the organization's purpose and the well-being of followers
- Create and sustain peace in the organization[469]

Humility. Philippians 2:17, in which Paul described his "pouring out as a libation." Paul was in jail for preaching the gospel at the time of his writing. He placed everything about himself less important than the message that Jesus is Lord, even to the point of incarceration. Through Paul's writing, it is obvious he placed the needs of Jesus's followers first. He encouraged, enlightened, and taught no matter what his circumstances. In Philippians 2:3, Paul urged the followers, "Do nothing from selfish ambition or concept; in humility regard others as better than yourselves." He also pointed to Jesus's example of the humility of death on the cross in verse 8.

Concern for others. In Philippians 2:4, Paul says, "Look not to your own interests but to the interests of others." Showing and modeling compassion are two primary tenets of servant leadership, which include compassion and sympathy. Sendjaya and Sarros describe servant leadership's compassion as placing others' needs above your own, showing followers' concern for well-being and personal development.[470] Paul continuously modeled this behavior in action with his travels to and correspondence with the churches in the New Testament.

Controlled discipline. Controlled discipline is demonstrated in Philippians 2:12–16. Paul encouraged the Philippians to obey him

---

[469] Winston and Patterson 2006.
[470] Sendjaya and Sarros 2002.

in his absence as they did in his presence. He reminded them that God is at work to enable them to be disciplined in their will (meaning their intent) and their work (meaning their actions and what they do). Jesus also maintained controlled discipline in verses 6–8. Through obedience to the will of God the Father, Jesus fulfilled His task and purpose on earth. This also applies to servant leadership in that leaders are focused and in control of their actions and emotions. Leaders set the example, encourage, edify, and discipline as needed to bring peace when interacting with others.

Seek what is right and good for the organization. Through the unity expressed in verses 1 to 4, Paul expresses how vital it is for the Philippians to seek commonality through sharing in the Spirit, the same mind, the same love, being of the full accord, and of one mind. In verses 14 to 16, Paul encouraged the Philippian church to exemplify what is good and right, not only for the sharing of the gospel but as an example to those who remain part of the material culture. Servant leaders seek out the right and the good for individuals under their leadership, which also bolsters the good of the organization.

Focus on the organization's purpose and the well-being of followers. Jesus showed mercy through His death on the cross. He knew He was sacrificing everything for the good of all through His death and resurrection. He showed mercy and compassion with humility and obedience. Servant leaders who show mercy enhance the relationship between themselves and their followers. There is also a level of trust that increases through mercy. Mercy does not negate accountability; it brings in a level of generosity that encourages individuals to do what is right, focusing on the organization's purpose and followers' well-being.

Although Paul was jailed, the gospel was his focus and purpose. He encouraged the Philippians to keep the unity of the gospel as the focus of their lives. Throughout Philippians 2:1–18, Paul encouraged them to look out for one another—with compassion and mercy, without argument or selfishness—so that they could shine like stars in the dark culture of their day. The same holds for servant leaders in any organization today. Every organization has a mission statement and a purpose that guides the organization. Servant leaders work toward the organization's goal and mission while integrating followers' well-being into the plan. Servant leaders dedicate themselves to serving the people who accomplish the tasks and purposes of the organization. Paul alluded to this aspect of servant leadership in verses 3 to 4: "regarding others better than yourselves" and looking "to the interests of others."

Create and sustain peace in the organization. Finally, Paul told the Philippian church not to murmur or argue amongst themselves, to be blameless and innocent, children of God (Philippians 2:14–15). The peace between each other that Paul spoke of is an example to the rest of the world. He desired to see the church have peace amongst themselves, which would not happen with arguments and murmuring between each other. Creating and sustaining peace within an organization is difficult because of the many personalities, ambitions, and motives converging in one place. The servant leader discerns conflict areas and works toward peaceful resolution between individuals and the organization. As Paul demonstrated to the Philippians, the servant leader also seeks to grow peace within the organization through relationship development, encouragement, and improvement.

Paul's demonstration of the principles of servant leadership is an example of a practical application within a specific organization that also transcends culture and time. Philippians 2:1–18 lays a solid foundation for applying servant-leadership principles, which focus on improving and encouraging followers while meeting the organization's goals. Servant leaders maintain a strong sense of self-awareness and spiritual awareness that aid in understanding themselves and the impacts of their actions on others.[471] Paul's example of Jesus's humility and obedience clarifies those living in times when morality, ethics, and values are questioned, mocked, or rejected as they were during Jesus's and Paul's lives. The illumination of a scriptural basis for servant leadership in Philippians 2:1–18 strengthens the worth and value of serving others through leadership. Servant leadership is a dynamic, engaging paradox that is the peace of connection between leader and follower.

---

[471] Song 2018.

Peace of Connection

Who you are

Internal peace comes from knowing who you are inside. It is part of self-awareness, which is your ability to identify and know your emotions and moods, what causes them, and how they affect others. Your peace comes from knowing who you are on the inside and living it on the outside. When you are at peace within, you can regulate your emotions and control disruptive impulses or moods. You also have the motivation and passion for doing work in pursuit of goals with energy and persistence.

What you have

With peace comes empathy, which is an understanding of the emotions of others. You can relate to them and have a rapport that allows you to network with others. You have internal resources that make you resilient, curious, and want to go beyond perceived limitations. You know you have a calling and purpose in your life that brings creativity and strength.

How to walk

Dietrich Bonhoeffer said,

> There is no way to peace along the way of safety. For peace must be dared, it is the great venture and can never be safe. Peace is the opposite of security. To demand guarantees is to want to protect oneself.[472]

---

[472] Bonhoeffer 1998.

Walking in peace is a posture of the heart. It is living out your values authentically from the heart, living with others through respect, and demonstrating that you are who you say you are.

Scriptures

> I leave the gift of peace with you—my peace. Not the kind of fragile peace given by the world, but my perfect peace. Do not yield to fear or be troubled in your hearts—instead, be courageous. John 14:27 TPT)

> Do not be pulled in different directions or worried about a thing. Be saturated in prayer throughout each day, offering your faith-filled requests before God with overflowing gratitude. Tell him every detail of your life, then God's wonderful peace that transcends human understanding will make the answers known to you through Jesus Christ. (Philippians 4:6–7 TPT)

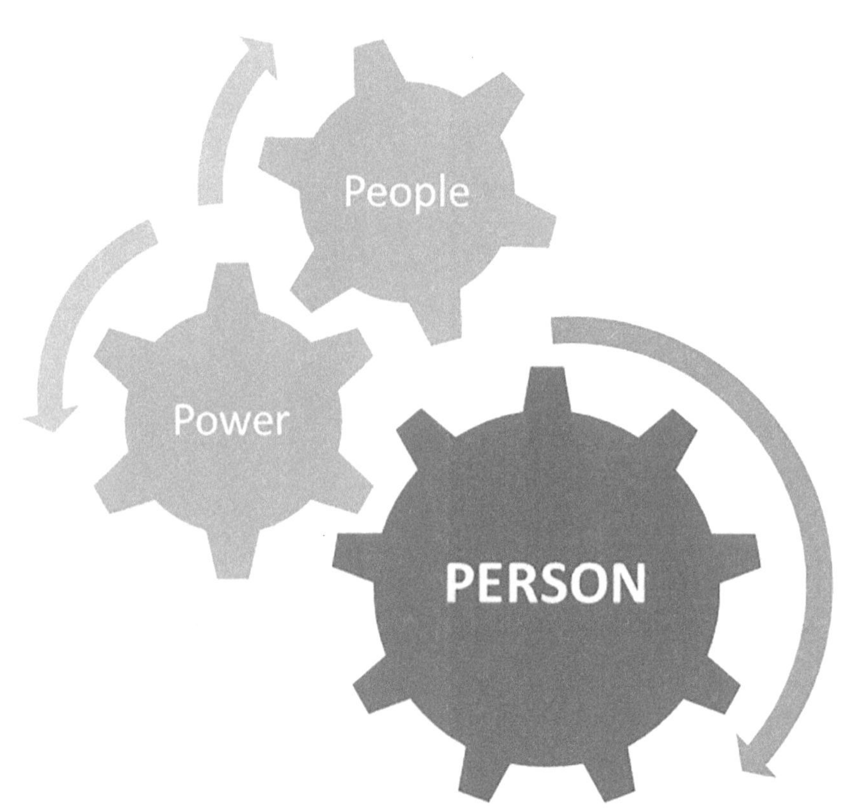
People
Power
PERSON

CHAPTER 6

Person of Connection

Jesus is the ultimate leader in style, grace, and strategy. He used several methods and strategies to train and prepare His followers to be leaders after He ascended to the Father. Jesus lived and taught love, peace, grace, and truth; showed compassion; and modeled servant leadership. In John 21:15–17 (NASB), Jesus asked Peter three times if he loved Him and to feed His sheep. Jesus knew He would leave soon after and wanted to ensure Peter cared for the new believers. Servant leadership is a bit of an oxymoron; it places others ahead of themselves rather than leading from the front.[473] In John 13:4–5 (NASB), Jesus modeled this concept for His disciples when He stooped to wash their feet. He said, "I am here to serve you," yet He still led them with teaching, confidence, and authority rooted in His relationship with Father God.

Jesus served the Father. Everything He did was with an awareness of serving Father God. He stated, "I do nothing without the Father" (John 5:30 NASB). Jesus also taught His followers to think, to be prepared with answers, to know why they served Him, and how to teach others to serve. His parables were relatable to the day's events, and He used them to help His followers find solutions to people's questions. Leaders relate to others through empathy, empower-

---

[473] Sen and Sarros 2002.

ing their followers versus demanding or telling.[474] Empowerment is a cornerstone of servant leadership.

In John 8, Jesus showed great compassion to the woman caught in adultery (John 8:3–10 NASB) and the Samaritan woman at the well (John 4:27–30 NASB). In both cases, Jesus demonstrated love and compassion as a servant leader. He could have condemned them and let them suffer punishment. His compassion was remarkable, and they received Him and went on to follow Him.[475] He gave the women something of Himself, and in turn, they were loyal to Him. Jesus was also true to Himself, the Father, and His followers. He is the essence of truth, which is the hallmark of authenticity.[476] He never pretends to be something He is not and never tries to influence His followers with anything less than authenticity.

The power of the Holy Spirit in us, the choice to follow Jesus, enables us to be servant leaders like Jesus. As Christians, we are charged to bring heaven to earth continually. Jesus told His disciples to preach that the kingdom of heaven is at hand (Matthew 10:7 NASB). We do not need an organization when we live from the inside out, from the Holy Spirit within us. However, organizations need servant leaders.

Impacting organizations

Organizations employ individuals with their thoughts, talents, skills, and abilities. Some are leaders; some are followers. We are in the world to serve, lead, mentor, and teach others through our example of Christ in us. Christian values can shape an organization's culture.[477] It is essential to know those values that align with Scripture and the ones that do not align so we can continually improve as a leader. Paul states in 1 Corinthians 2:12–13 (NASB) that we have received the Spirit from God and not the spirit of the world and that his teaching was from the Holy Spirit and not from human wisdom.

---

[474] Van Dierendonck and Patterson 2015.

[475] Davenport 2015.

[476] Van Dierendonck and Patterson 2015.

[477] Hultman and Gellerman 2002.

As we continually refine our leadership abilities, we have the examples and teachings from Jesus, His disciples, and the Holy Spirit that guide us into the truth of all things. In Christian enterprises, Spirit-led, Spirit-filled leaders are more impactful than unregenerate leaders with natural talents.[478] Considering this, we—as Spirit-led, Spirit-filled leaders—can influence an organization's culture in positive, Christ-centered ways as servant leaders.

Responsible leadership is when leaders look for the best standards for the organization and what is suitable for individuals.[479] Responsible leadership encourages individuals to achieve higher, and as a responsible leader, "pursuit of the highest good is a worthy aspiration."[480] Responsible leadership upholds the Golden Rule of seeking out the best in others as the leader wants the best brought out in him or herself. Leadership development is an ongoing process that requires consistent dedication, evaluation, and cultivation.[481] Leaders who learn and improve their leadership abilities earn additional trust and respect from followers.

Leadership as part of a lifestyle and worldview is an intriguing way of seeing biblical leadership. Jesus modeled sacrificial and servant leadership by placing the needs of followers above His own. Four servant-leadership traits are: empowering followers, stewardship, authenticity, and providing direction.[482] Jesus showed each trait through His interactions with His disciples and through His compassionate love for humanity.

New Testament

Paul also demonstrates the traits of servant leadership throughout his writings in the New Testament. He consistently writes to fellow believers, always praying, always with a spirit of love. In Colossians 1:9–12 (NASB), Paul shows authenticity by telling the

---

[478] Engstrom 1976.
[479] Cameron 2011.
[480] Cameron 2011.
[481] Engstrom 1976.
[482] Van Dierendonck and Patterson 2015.

believers that they are always in his prayers for wisdom and strength and their walk in a manner worthy of the Lord. Paul's compassionate love shines through in his description of Jesus, and he rejoices to see the Colossians have good discipline and stability of faith in Christ (Colossians 2:5). He provides them direction and guidance in maintaining faith in Christ and not allowing worldly philosophy and empty deception deceive them.

Paul was also interested in transforming lives through the knowledge and understanding of Jesus's death and resurrection. Cooper suggests that dynamic growth occurs when leadership encourages transformation[483] Growth also happens when the leader shares the vision with followers and works with followers to fulfill that vision. Paul influenced the culture, which changed remarkably during his lifetime. His dedication and sacrifice to "make known the riches of the glory of this mystery among the Gentiles, which is Christ in you, the hope of glory" (Colossians 1:27 NASB) provided a model for living. Through the example of Paul's love of Christ, we can learn to empower followers, steward our relationships wisely, be authentic, and provide direction to those who follow.

Christian leaders are called to "walk in a manner worthy of the calling…with humility, grace, tolerance, and love, diligently preserving the unity of the Spirit in the bond of peace" (Ephesians 4:1–3 NASB). Without the Holy Spirit within, guiding and equipping us, we would walk as the world and try to accomplish things independently.

Providing direction and addressing challenges apply to all leaders and are seen in various leaders in the Bible.[484] When King David encountered Goliath, he knew the Lord was with him and did not falter. He showed the people how to meet the challenge directly with God. His confidence and courage gave direction and inspiration to Israel so they could defeat the Philistines (1 Samuel 17). When we approach challenges in the same way, we show our followers that

---

[483] Cooper 2005.
[484] Northouse 2019.

overcoming a challenge or difficulty is possible, despite evidence to the contrary, but only when we maintain our relationship with God.

Transforming leadership

Our relationship with God is also what transforms us as leaders. Momeny and Gourgues state that Christian leaders need leadership education that transforms much like grace through faith transforms believers.[485] Christian leaders need biblical examples for education, inspiration, and transformation in their leadership abilities. Leadership training varies from leader to leader and with individual positions and experiences.[486] The result of any training should be a transformation of the leader. Paul and Peter's transformation and transformational leadership show us what this looks like. The question is how to develop transformational-leadership principles into practical training that transforms Christian leaders today.

Biblical leadership principles transcend culture and time and apply to leadership challenges experienced in all areas of life.[487] From a biblical perspective, servant-leadership principles and traits place individuals and relationships ahead of the organization or community but do not exclude the organization's goals. Aligning individual and organizational goals and objectives creates a mutually beneficial and dynamic relationship. Paul's example of servant leadership applied to every community and culture he encountered. Biblical servant-leader principles transcend time to present-day leaders, organizations, and communities. When servant leaders empower individuals, they can add significance to the organization with internal values, principles, and relationships. The organizational culture and context also influence servant leadership in applying external manifestations.[488] Actions appropriate to the organization or industry are essential considerations in servant leadership.

---

[485] Momeny and Gourgues 2019.
[486] Ibid.
[487] Bell 2014.
[488] Northouse 2019.

When actioning the principles of servant leadership, the outcomes include personal growth and performance, organizational performance, and societal impact.[489] The results of servant leadership empower followers and maximize their potential. In turn, empowered followers contribute to enhanced organizational performance, positively impacting society. Servant-leadership principles are, in a sense, perpetual because they do not stop with the individual. The results affect many areas of society and culture.

With a selfless mindset, servant leaders carry influence in any area and industry. The servant leader focuses on the individual and leads them in growth and development, positively impacting the organization.[490] Servant leaders operate from knowing who they are; their purpose is to serve and lead. Servant leadership is a calling that proceeds from the inside out.[491] Service comes from the heart, from a position of love to the outside, demonstrated through service. When the servant also leads, it comes from love and a desire to uplift, provoke, and propel followers to their best selves. In Mark 10:43 (TPT), Jesus says, "You are to lead by a different model. If you want to be the greatest one, live as one called to serve others." Jesus's example was of servant leadership rather than the example of leaders who ruled by oppression.

Servant leaders apply listening and compassion skills to build trusting relationships with followers to empower them.[492] Empowerment requires continuous growth and development by encouraging and activating individual talent.[493] Servant leaders also help followers develop a vision and align thinking and outcomes that help fulfill the vision.[494] Servant leadership combines humility and behaviors that encourage action and efficacy.[495] Humility shows a

---

[489] Ibid.
[490] Coetzer et al. 2017.
[491] Bell and Habel 2010.
[492] Coetzer et al. 2017.
[493] Ibid.
[494] Bell and Habel 2010.
[495] Sousa and Van Dierendonck 2017.

willingness to place others ahead of self, giving support and credit to uplift and encourage.[496]

From a biblical perspective, servant leadership proceeds from the inside out, from knowing who you are in Christ and serving from that position. Jesus lived from the inside out, knowing who His Father was and operating in His mission and calling. In John 8:28, Jesus says He does nothing on His initiative but only what He sees the Father doing. Seven virtuous constructs that define servant leadership are agape love, humility, altruism, vision, trust, empowerment, and service.[497] The virtues of servant leadership must be practiced through relationships, just as Jesus had a relationship with the Father. Jesus's relationship with the Father modeled the way that defines, affirms, and aligns actions with shared values.[498]

Love in leadership

In the letter to the Corinthian church, Paul covers various topics. First Corinthians 13, considered the love chapter, expounds on the foundation of love that strengthens the servant-leadership model. Leadership is grounded in love.[499] First Corinthians 13:4–7 lists the actions of love: patience, kindness, forgiving, truth, forbearance, belief, hope, and endurance. The actions of a servant leader support followers with love from the heart. Servant leaders desire to serve others, help them achieve goals, and become more than they thought possible.[500] Love is an action supporting and building others through service.

The agape love Paul describes is practical for transforming lives, reconciling relationships, and producing good fruit individually and corporately.[501] Paul reminded the Corinthian church that their actions and decisions influenced believers and unbelievers. Paul's

---

[496] Ibid.

[497] Patterson 2003.

[498] Kouzes and Posner 2017.

[499] Bell 2014.

[500] Whittington et al. 2005.

[501] Bell 2014.

reminder applies to servant leadership today. Servant leaders who teach, train, and mentor with love set aside selfish gain and ambition to help develop followers and influence the next generation of servant leaders.[502] Organizations that recognize and incorporate servant-leadership training help nurture emotional intelligence, ethical decision-making, and empowering skills.[503] Practical application of servant leadership founded on love bears fruit from the individual to the organization and surrounding community.

Paul had the daunting task of changing the minds and culture of the Corinthian believers. Their hearts were changed by the love of Jesus and the desire to follow His example. Their minds had to renew (Romans 12:2), which would help change the culture of believers and then the rest of the city. The church leaders in Corinth needed to think and act differently than the secular leaders to set an example for others. Paul's letters highlighted areas of needed correction, with much encouragement and solid teaching applicable today.

Contemporary servant leaders must also follow Paul's leadership techniques when leading others. Leaders walking in authenticity and integrity cannot be afraid to correct followers when needed, always with love and encouragement. Authenticity and integrity are not exclusive to the church or any other organization. Servant leaders carry these qualities and live them from the inside out. It is a way of life, built on a foundation of love in Christ Jesus, that servant leaders walk out and demonstrate no matter where they go and whom they encounter. Leadership is a relational process having less to do with position and more with community and relationships God has placed in our path.[504]

Servant leadership as a lifelong process helps define a legacy and trains the next generation of servant leaders. Excellence in Christian leadership is a process that requires constant evaluation, correction, and improvement.[505] The process is what Paul describes in the letters to the Corinthians. In 1 Corinthians 9:24–27, Paul speaks of the pro-

---

[502] Crowther 2018.
[503] Northouse 2019.
[504] Bell 2014.
[505] Engstrom 1976.

cess involving self-control, discipline, training, direction, and vision. The servant-leader process also depends on those four categories to develop the leader within and then pass that process to followers.

As mentors, servant leaders combine organizational-specific training with relationships and follower development.[506] The mentorship process can change lives to reflect love, care, and concern to the mentor.[507] When followers become leaders, they, in turn, change lives with the love, care, and concern they were shown.[508] Mentorship for the servant leader also includes a continuous process of internal improvement. Mentoring followers through self-improvement, goals, foresight, skill-building, and community relationships also empowers followers.[509] With empowerment also comes responsibility.

Paul discusses accountability in 2 Corinthians 13:1–3. In this third reminder, he reminds the believers again that sin is not tolerated and that even through weakness, the power of God within enables strength. Paul's example applies to servant leaders and followers for accountability. Servant leaders are accountable for their actions, just as followers are accountable for their actions.[510] Accountability helps build the relationship between leader and follower while encouraging each other to uphold values and morals. Accountability also helps leaders and followers maintain excellence throughout the leadership process.[511] As Paul (2 Corinthians 13:10), accountability is for building up and not tearing down.

Jesus's model of servant leadership was direct: "Greater love has no man than to lay down his life for another." Jesus was the archetype of servant leadership. His direct relationship and connection with Father God was the model His followers would emulate. His model of servant leadership was perfect. Jesus reminded His disciples that self-sacrifice on behalf of those in need is necessary (Mark 10:45).[512]

---

[506] Pearson 2012.
[507] Whittington et al. 2005.
[508] Ibid.
[509] Murari and Gupta 2012.
[510] Northouse 2019.
[511] Engstrom 1976.
[512] Agosto 2005.

Jesus presented the theory and principles of servant leadership to His disciples, who then put His principles into action, as in Acts 2:45, when the followers of Jesus shared with those in need.

Model servant leadership

Paul's servant-leadership model developed after encountering Jesus on the road to Damascus. Paul said in Galatians 1:11–12 that he received the gospel directly from Jesus. His apostolic task was to preach the gospel of Jesus to the Gentiles. After his conversion, Paul preached the gospel for three years before he met the disciples in Jerusalem. Paul also traveled extensively, encountering many cultures, tribes, and nations. Everywhere he went, Paul taught with authority given to him by Jesus. His message included service before self and addressed issues and concerns in the context of the culture. When Paul discusses the gifts of the Spirit in 1 Corinthians 12, he reminds the Corinthians that gifts are for the members of the body, not to glorify themselves but in service to one another. Leadership is a relational and community process.[513]

Paul's servant-leadership model also included the transformation of self in pursuit of personal growth while serving others. He encouraged the followers of Jesus to serve each other, those with whom they shared the gospel. Paul demonstrated practical actions of servant leadership that others could model up to the contemporary church and organizations. Contemporary leaders can learn insights and principles from Paul that apply to organizational ethics, values, and vision to create a shared service goal within the organization and the community.[514] Servant-leadership principles can be taught and developed in a contemporary organization.[515]

Servant leaders choose first to serve then lead. Choosing to serve comes from compassionate love.[516] The question is how a leader chooses service over power, especially if the leader began from

---

[513] Bell 2014.
[514] Ibid.
[515] Northouse 2019.
[516] Van Dierendonck and Patterson 2015.

a position of power. In Paul's example, he was in a position of power as a Pharisee. He was zealously committed to keeping Jewish law and persecuting the new church (Philippians 3:5–6). However, Paul encountered Jesus on the Damascus road (Acts 9:3–6) and converted from an influential Pharisee leader to a servant of Jesus. In Galatians 1:13–16, Paul says he was set apart by God, from his mother's womb, called by His grace, and God was pleased to reveal His Son in him to preach to the Gentiles.

The transformation from leader to servant happens when the leader realizes Jesus within. In Galatians 2:20 (NASB), Paul says, "It is no longer I who live, but Christ lives in me." He also reiterates that Jesus loved him and gave Himself up for him. When Jesus is the leader's heart, service becomes more important than position. The leader can then learn how to display love, cultivate community, and communicate the meaning of work.[517] Paul influenced those he taught by modeling servant-leader behavior rather than asserting power over the followers.[518] Paul demonstrated and taught with authenticity and sincerity, demonstrating other servant-leadership qualities.

Paul's leadership model also focuses on follower development.[519] Paul encourages followers with a shared vision and motivation to transform the inner person consistent with Jesus's teachings. When the leader moves from power to service, the follower's growth and development lead to the organization's growth.[520] Paul's leadership changed from power to service, and through his model and example, the early church experienced growth that continues through the modern servant leaders.

Servant leaders take action

Servant leadership is more than completing acts of service. It is important to remember that servant leadership starts with choosing

---

[517] Dean 2019.
[518] Whittington et al. 2005.
[519] Ibid.
[520] Crowther 2018.

to serve and lead.[521] Service places the needs of others before self, just as Jesus put the needs of humanity before Himself. Servant leadership also includes leading others into growth and development. With the application of servant leadership, the practices can become: model the way as a servant leader, inspire a shared servant-leader vision, change the process to servant leadership, empower followers in servant leadership, and encourage the heart of followers as a servant leader.

In addition, servant leaders can empower employees to think, behave, act, control work, and make decisions to encourage employees to take ownership of themselves and their contributions to the organization.[522] Servant leaders who empower followers through foresight, persuasion, awareness, and stewardship impact individuals and organizational performance.[523] Jesus clarified that true leadership is grounded in love, which must be addressed in service.[524]

Paul's experience as a persecutor, a tyrannical leader, gave him a perspective he used to show the dangers of leadership without love and regard for followers. His example is extreme to contemporary leaders, but the teaching and model show how a leader focuses on self and power, leading to pride, arrogance, and a fall. However, God intervened and demonstrated that His saving grace is more than sufficient to change the heart of a leader into one of a servant.

Persecution also increases the church's resilience and determination to preach the gospel of Jesus. Knowing God was understood through experience: trusting Him and His faithfulness during persecution.[525] As Paul says, "All who desire to live godly in Christ Jesus will be persecuted" (2 Timothy 3:12). Despite persecution, the church—followers of Jesus, empowered by the Holy Spirit—is internally driven to love and bear witness to the gospel of Jesus.[526] Leaders in contemporary churches must serve their followers from within

---

[521] Greenleaf 1977.

[522] Murari and Gupta 2012.

[523] Ibid.

[524] Enstrom 1976.

[525] Zaprometova 2018.

[526] Kipfer 2017.

through the love of Jesus. Persecution can be a tool to build resilience and empower followers to understand the strength they have in Christ.

The most crucial issue contemporary servant leaders face is the understanding that we serve God by leading others in love. Again, Psalm 23 (NASB) shows God leading and serving us because of His great love for us, not because of anything we have done or accomplished. He does it because He is love. We can be steward leaders, caring, loving, and leading others from God's vision.[527] It can also be called spiritual leadership in which God gives leaders a vision to steward and carry so that as servant leaders, we can impact people, organizations, and communities.[528] Every leader in the Old Testament began with God as the true leader, who gave them a vision, stewarded the vision, and led others in the fulfillment of the vision.

Honesty and integrity are essential qualities of excellent leadership, evident in the consistency of motives, character, and conduct.[529] Proverbs 10:9 (NASB) states, "He who walks in integrity walks securely. But he who perverts his ways will be found out." Integrity is a fundamental biblical principle. Leaders should have integrity as part of their moral code to be credible and effective.[530] Integrity is part of character orientation, which focuses on developing a servant's attitude with values, credibility, and motive.[531]

Mentoring the next generation of leaders is an essential component of servant leadership: the servant leader sacrifices for the life of one's children.[532] Servant leadership goes beyond self-promotion and emphasizes building up the next leader or generation of leaders. Isaiah 53:6 says all of us are sheep gone astray and turned to our way. As mentors, servant leaders can guide, teach, and train the next

---

[527] Rodin 2013.
[528] Bell 2014, Coetzer et al. 2017.
[529] Engstrom 1978
[530] Oncken 2000
[531] Bell and Habel 2010.
[532] Moore 2007.

generation of leaders in the direction they should go.[533] The direction must come from the highest authority and wisdom, which is God.

Servant leaders understand the impact of imparting knowledge and experience into the life of another, which creates a legacy in individuals, organizations, and societies.[534] Servant leaders influence and help others reach their full potential.[535] Just as God focuses on people rather than institutions and organizations, servant leaders focus on the individual, changing the organization's culture and creating value for all.[536] Isaiah demonstrated mentorship through his work as a prophet to forward God's vision for future generations.

Leaders must know who they are, what they have, and how to walk in it. Leadership authority comes from God, the Creator, who gave dominion over humankind over the earth. Dominion brings a responsibility to nurture and care for creation in a way that reflects the image of God.[537] Leaders also need to know and understand what they have as an image bearer of God. They carry the image of a loving, creative God with intelligence, wisdom, and a capacity for innovation and love for all creation.

Moreover, leaders must know how to walk in a manner worthy of their life's calling. As Paul implores us in Ephesians 4:1–3 (NASB),

> Walk in a manner worthy of the calling
> with which you have been called, with humility
> and gentleness, with patience, showing tolerance
> for one another in love, being diligent to preserve
> the unity of the Spirit in the bond of peace.

As leaders, our relationships with people are the most important. Jesus held people accountable and did not remind them of their sins every minute. Essentially, He said, "I see what you did. I forgive you. Go and sin no more." As leaders, we are responsible for holding

---

[533] Engstrom 1976.

[534] Pearson 2012.

[535] Ibid.

[536] Coetzer et al. 2017.

[537] Towner 2005.

people accountable for their actions and providing grace and mercy to allow them to correct their actions and move forward as Jesus did. Organizations employ individuals with their thoughts, talents, skills, and abilities. Some are leaders; some are followers. We are in the world to serve, lead, mentor, and teach others through our example of Christ in us. Christian values can shape an organization's culture.[538] It is essential to know those values that align with Scripture and the ones that do not align so we can continually improve as a leader. Paul states in 1 Corinthians 2:12–13(NASB) that we have received the Spirit from God and not the spirit of the world and that his teaching was from the Holy Spirit and not from human wisdom.

As we continually refine our leadership abilities, we have the examples and teachings from Jesus, His disciples, and the Holy Spirit that guide us into the truth of all things. In Christian enterprises, Spirit-led, Spirit-filled leaders are more impactful than unregenerate leaders with natural talents.[539] Considering this, we—as Spirit-led, Spirit-filled leaders—can influence an organization's culture in positive, Christ-centered ways as servant leaders.

Person of Connection

Who you are

Mastering leadership within causes us to ask humble questions that illuminate answers. The answers we seek are found in the faith in the truth that gives us an advantage over what we see. With self-awareness, we have internalized moral reasoning and know what to do when things are unclear. We spiritually connect with God through Jesus to explore and live out an intimate relationship with God that comes with joy, peace, contentment, and fulfillment of an abundant life.

---

[538] Hultman and Gellerman 2002.
[539] Engstrom 1976.

What you have

When you know who you are in Christ, you have love within you that connects you with others. You have peace through everything, including failures. You are equipped with perseverance and resilience that provides the push you need to keep moving into your destiny. You have a loving mindset that gives you a posture of servant leadership and strengthens you for the good works God has prepared for you.

How to walk

Leading is risky. It is placing yourself in a position of self-examination and self-sacrifice to walk through confrontations in truth and love. You advocate for those who cannot advocate for themselves. You are a builder, bridging gaps and connecting people to their moment to shine in the light. As a leader, you look for the best in those searching for significance. They may not recall what you did, but they will remember how you made them feel. Walk in love.

Scripture

> Love is large and incredibly patient. Love is gentle and consistently kind to all. It refuses to be jealous when a blessing comes to someone else. Love does not brag about one's achievements nor inflate its own importance. Love does not traffic in shame and disrespect nor selfishly seek its own honor. Love is not easily irritated or quick to take offense. Love joyfully celebrates honesty and finds no delight in what is wrong. Love is a safe place of shelter, for it never stops believing in the best for others. Love never takes failure as defeat, for it never gives up. (1 Corinthians 13:4–7 TPT)

CONCLUSION

Actions of a Leader: Know Who You Are

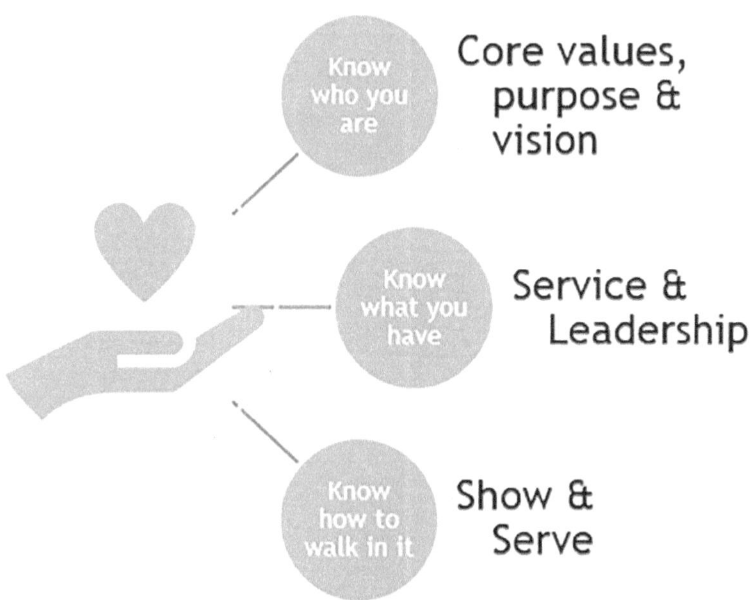

Character

- Internal values
- Integrity
- Humility

- Self-awareness
- Motives
- Honest
- Attitude

Leaders always look to improve themselves internally to be better leaders every day. They are willing to do the hard work that helps them follow a path of personal growth that inspires others to act.

Unethical actions affect your leadership, as well. Followers who see your actions have several choices regarding you as a leader. They can choose to follow your immoral behavior, thereby perpetuating an unethical culture in the organization. Followers can decide you are not acting as an excellent ethical leader and decide not to follow your leadership, which is detrimental to morale and unit cohesion.

Leaders have a responsibility to their followers, like it or not, and the example a leader sets can influence a follower for years to come.

Actions of a Leader: Know What You Have

Skills

- Relationship
- Vision
- Trust
- Communicate
- Engage
- Develop
- Humility

Leaders inspire others to achieve excellence and go higher than they thought possible. Leaders pave the way for others to follow through example, encouragement, and excellence. Nevertheless, they can only do this if their leadership and life demonstrate ethics and morality.

Leaders must communicate and engage followers to improve and grow an ethical culture in their organization. Leaders must also acknowledge when they are wrong and take action to rectify the wrong. Leaders with humility also show followers that internal growth and development are continuous and sometimes humbling processes.

Actions of a Leader: How to Walk in It

Demonstrate

- Service
- Vision
- Influence
- Mentor
- Teach
- Empowerment
- Steward

Be an example of the kind of leader you may not have had. Be teachable to gain wisdom and understanding of yourself. Serve others with grace, teach, and train as you go. Leaders influence followers either positively or negatively. A good leader who cares for followers understands that service is part of leadership development and includes a process of empowerment through self-awareness, self-control, and self-reflection. The leader's strength comes from the foundation of core values and beliefs. A leader wisely stewards a leadership vision and foundation others can follow to become wise leaders.

Your leadership foundation comes from knowing what you have. In other words, it comes from your core values and beliefs. Your core values and beliefs are those you live by personally and professionally. They show others the right way to live and that you have internal knowledge and confidence that enables you to carry out your leadership duties and responsibilities.

Leaders with a foundation of core values and beliefs know they can draw upon these regularly. Leaders balance their core values and beliefs with their decisions without compromising ethics. Leaders act and walk out their core values and beliefs through ethical choices, actions, and relationships with others. Leaders live like no one else by putting others before themselves through making ethical decisions and choices, personally and professionally. It takes a conscious effort to live out core values and beliefs. The world needs examples of noble, moral people who are willing to maintain the foundation of their core values and beliefs.

WORKS CITED

Ackermann, Fran, and Colin Eden. 2011. *Making Strategy: Mapping Out Strategic Success*. London: SAGE.

Adair, John Eric. 2007. *Leadership for Innovation: How to Organise Team Creativity and Harvest Ideas*. London: Kogan Page.

Agosto, Efrain. 2005. *Servant Leadership: Jesus & Paul*. St. Louis, MO: Chalice Press.

Amis, John M., and Royston Greenwood. 2021. "Organisational Change in a (Post-) Pandemic World: Rediscovering Interests and Values." *Journal of Management Studies* 58, no. 2: 582–6.

Anderson, Dianna L., and Merrill C. Anderson. 2005. *Coaching That Counts: Harnessing the Power of Leadership Coaching to Deliver Strategic Value*. Amsterdam: Elsevier/Butterworth-Heinemann.

Anderson, Robert J., and W. A. Adams. 2015. *Mastering Leadership: An Integrated Framework for Breakthrough Performance and Extraordinary Business Results*. Hoboken, NJ: Wiley.

Andersson, Thomas, et al. 2019. "Building Traits for Organizational Resilience through Balancing Organizational Structures." *Scandinavian Journal of Management* 35, no. 1: 36–45.

Argenti, Paul A. 2004. "Collaborating with Activists: How Starbucks Works with NGOs." *California Management Review* 47, no. 1: 91–116.

Avolio, Bruce J., et al. 2004. *Unlocking the Mask: A Look at the Process by which Authentic Leaders Impact Follower Attitudes and Behaviors* 15.

Avolio, Bruce J., Fred O. Walumbwa, and Todd J. Weber. 2009. "Leadership: Current Theories, Research, and Future Directions." *Annual Review of Psychology* 60, no. 1: 421–49.

Badaracco, Joseph. 1997. *Defining Moments: When Managers Must Choose between Right and Right.* Boston, MA: Harvard Business School Press.

Bajaba, Abdulah, et al. 2021. "Adaptive Managers as Emerging Leaders during the COVID-19 Crisis." *Frontiers in Psychology* 12: 661628.

Baldoni, John. 2003. *Great Communication Secrets of Great Leaders.* New York: McGraw-Hill.

Banerjee, Pratyush, and Sweta Singh. 2015. "Managers' Perspectives on the Effects of Online Grapevine Communication: A Qualitative Inquiry." *The Qualitative Report* 20, no. 6: 765.

Banks, Amy. 2011. "Developing the Capacity to Connect." *Zygon* 46, no. 1: 168–82.

Barentsen, Jack. 2018. "The Social Construction of Paul's Apostolic Leadership in Corinth." *HTS Teologiese Studies* 74, no. 4.

Barnes, Sandra L., Angela Cowser, and Terrick A. Gutierrez. 2017. "Leadership Amidst Poverty: A Mixed-Methodological Analysis of the Shack Dweller Federation of Namibia." *Journal of African American Studies* 21, no. 2: 216–35.

Bass, Bernard M., and Paul Steidlmeier. 1999. "Ethics, Character, and Authentic Transformational Leadership Behavior." *The Leadership Quarterly* 10, no. 2: 181–217.

Bazerman, Max H., and Ann E. Tenbrunsel. 2011. *Blind Spots: Why We Fail to Do What's Right and What to Do About It.* Princeton, NJ: Princeton University Press.

Beerel, Annabel. 1997. "The Strategic Planner as Prophet and Leader: A Case Study Concerning a Leading Seminary Illustrates the New Planning Skills Required." *Leadership & Organization Development Journal* 18, no. 3: 136–44.

Bell, Michael, and Sylvia Habel. 2010. "Enacting Servant-Leadership from the Inside Out." *The International Journal of Servant-Leadership* 6, no. 1: 213–34.

Bell, Skip. 2014. *Servants and Friends: A Biblical Theology of Leadership.* Andrews University Press.

Berkun, Scott. 2010. *The Myths of Innovation.* Sebastopol: O'Reilly.

Bielo, James S. 2012. "Belief, Deconversion, and Authenticity among U.S. Emerging Evangelicals." *Ethos* 40, no. 3: 258–76.

Block, Peter. 2011. *Flawless Consulting: A Guide to Getting Your Expertise Used.* Hoboken: Pfeiffer.

Bormann, Sara. 2020. "Strategic Priorities and Organizational Design." *Journal of Management Accounting Research* 32, no. 3: 7.

Boysen, Sheila, et al. 2018. "Organisational Coaching Outcomes: A Comparison of a Practitioner Survey and Key Findings from the Literature." *International Journal of Evidence-Based Coaching and Mentoring* 16, no. 1: 159–66.

Brown, Brené. 2022. *The Gifts of Imperfection.* Center City, MN: Hazelden Publishing.

Brown, Michael E., and Marie S. Mitchell. 2010. "Ethical and Unethical Leadership: Exploring New Avenues for Future Research." *Business Ethics Quarterly* 20, no. 4: 583–616.

Browne, Katherine E., Caela O'Connell, and Laura Meitzner Yoder. 2018. "Journey through the Groan Zone with Academics and Practitioners: Bridging Conflict and Difference to Strengthen Disaster Risk Reduction and Recovery Work." *International Journal of Disaster Risk Science* 9, no. 3: 421–8.

Burton, Richard M., and Børge Obel. 2018. "The Science of Organizational Design: Fit between Structure and Coordination." *Journal of Organization Design* 7, no. 1: 1–13.

Cabrera, Angel, and Gregory Unruh. 2012. *Being Global: How to Think, Act, and Lead in a Transformed World.* Boston, Mass: Harvard Business Review Press.

Caligiuri, Paula. 2006. "Developing Global Leaders." *Human Resource Management Review* 16, no. 2: 219–28.

———. 2012. *Cultural Agility: Building a Pipeline of Successful Global Professionals.* San Francisco, CA: Jossey-Bass.

Caligiuri, Paula, and Ibraiz Tarique. 2012. *Dynamic Cross-Cultural Competencies and Global Leadership Effectiveness.* 47.

Cameron, Kim S., and Robert E. Quinn. 2011. *Diagnosing and Changing Organizational Culture: Based on the Competing Values Framework.* San Francisco, CA: Jossey-Bass.

Cameron, Kim. 2011. "Responsible Leadership as Virtuous Leadership." *Journal of Business Ethics* 98, no. 1: 25–35.

Carmeli, Abraham, Yair Friedman, and Asher Tishler. 2013. "Cultivating a Resilient Top Management Team: The Importance of Relational Connections and Strategic Decision Comprehensiveness." *Safety Science* 51, no. 1: 148–59.

Carmeli, Abraham., R. Gelbard, and R. Reiter-Palmon. 2013. "Leadership, Creative Problem-Solving Capacity, and Creative Performance: The Importance of Knowledge Sharing." *Human Resource Management* 52, no. 1: 95–121.

Cerne, Matej, Marko Jaklic, and Miha Skerlavaj. 2013. "Authentic Leadership, Creativity, and Innovation: A Multilevel Perspective." *Leadership* 9, no. 1: 63–85.

Chatterjee, D. 2006. "Wise Ways: Leadership as Relationship." *Journal of Human Values* 12, no. 2: 153–160.

Citrin, Richard, and Alan Weiss. 2016. *The Resilience Advantage: Stop Managing Stress and Find Your Resilience*. New York, NY: Business Expert Press.

Ciulla, Joanne B., et al. 2018. "Guest Editors' Introduction: Philosophical Contributions to Leadership Ethics." *Business Ethics Quarterly* 28, no. 1: 1–14.

Coates, Joseph F. 2004. "Coming to Grips with the Future." *Research Technology Management* 47, no. 5: 23–32.

Coetzer, Michiel, Mark Bussin, and Madelyn Geldenhuys. 2017. "The Functions of a Servant Leader." *Administrative Sciences* 7, no. 1: 5.

Collins, Gary R. 2009. *Christian Coaching: Helping Others Turn Potential into Reality*. Colorado Springs, CO: NavPress.

Cooper, Michael. 2005. "The Transformational Leadership of the Apostle Paul: A Contextual and Biblical Leadership for Contemporary Ministry." *Christian Education Journal* 2, no. 1: 48–61.

Crampton, Suzanne M., John W. Hodge, and Jitendra M. Mishra. 1998. "The Informal Communication Network: Factors Influencing Grapevine Activity." *Public Personnel Management* 27, no. 4: 569–84.

Crowther, Steven. 2018. *Biblical Servant Leadership*. Cham: Springer International Publishing.

Cseh, Maria, Elizabeth B. Davis, and Shaista E. Khilji. 2013. "Developing a Global Mindset: Learning of Global Leaders." *European Journal of Training and Development* 37, no. 5: 489–99.

Davenport, Brian. 2015. "Compassion, Suffering and Servant-Leadership: Combining Compassion and Servant-Leadership to Respond to Suffering." *Leadership* 11, no. 3: 300–15.

Dean, D. 2019. "Integration of Christian Values in the Workplace." *Journal of Biblical Perspectives in Leadership* 9, no. 1 (Fall): 35–55.

De Lange, Lucrezea, and Dalmé Mulder. 2022. "Towards More Effective Leadership Communication." *Communicare: Journal for Communication Studies in Africa* 36, no. 1: 27–46.

DeSilva, D. A. 2018. *An Introduction to the New Testament: Contexts, Methods, and Ministry Formation*. Westmont: InterVarsity Press.

Department of Defense. 2021. "Annual Report on Suicide in the Military CY 2021 with CY21 DoDSER." Accessed March 6, 2022. https://www.dspo.mil/Portals/113/Documents/2022%20ASR/Annual%20Report%20on%20Suicide%20in%20the%20Military%20CY%202021%20with%20CY21%20DoDSER%20(1).pdf?ver=tat8FRrUhH2IlndFrCGbsA%3d%3d.

Duignan, Patrick A., and Narottam Bhindi. 1997. "Authenticity in Leadership: An Emerging Perspective." *Journal of Educational Administration* 35, no. 3: 195–209.

Engstrom, Theodore Wilhelm. 1976. *The Making of a Christian Leader*. Grand Rapids: Zondervan Pub. House.

Erden, Nil Selenay. 2013. "Power Distance Leads to Corporate Grapevine: The Mediating Role of Perceptions of Uncertainty." *Journal of Multidisciplinary Research* 5, no. 1: 95.

Fedler, Kyle D. 2006. *Exploring Christian Ethics: Biblical Foundations for Morality*. Louisville, KY: Westminster John Knox Press.

Felício, J. Augusto, Ieva Meidutė, and Øyvin Kyvik. 2016. "Global Mindset, Cultural Context, and the Internationalization of SMEs." *Journal of Business Research* 69, no. 11: 4924–32.

Flocco, Nicole, Filomena Canterino, and Raffaella Cagliano. 2022. "To Control or Not to Control: How to Organize Employee-Driven Innovation." *Creativity and Innovation Management* 31, no. 3: 396–409.

Forsyth, Bryan, and Kennedy Maranga. 2015. "Global Leadership Competencies and Training." *Journal of Leadership, Accountability and Ethics* 12, no. 5: 76–83.

Foss, Nicolai J. 2021. "The Impact of the COVID-19 Pandemic on Firms' Organizational Designs." *Journal of Management Studies* 58, no. 1: 268–72.

Gandolfi, Franco, Seth Stone, and Frank Deno. 2017. "Servant Leadership: An Ancient Style with 21st Century Relevance." *Revista de Management Comparat International* 18, no. 4: 350–61.

García-Morales, Víctor Jesús, María Magdalena Jiménez-Barrionuevo, and Leopoldo Gutiérrez-Gutiérrez. 2012. *Transformational Leadership Influence on Organizational Performance through Organizational Learning and Innovation*. 65.

Gardner, William L., B. J. Avolio, and Fred O. Walumbwa. 2005. *Authentic Leadership Theory and Practice: Origins, Effects, and Development*. Amsterdam, Netherlands: JAI Press Inc.

Gardner, William L., et al. 2005. *"Can You See the Real Me?" A Self-Based Model of Authentic Leader and Follower Development*. Vol. 16.

Gaspar, Rui, et al. 2016. "Beyond Positive or Negative: Qualitative Sentiment Analysis of Social Media Reactions to Unexpected Stressful Events." *Computers in Human Behavior* 56: 179–91.

George, Bill. 2003. *Authentic Leadership: Rediscovering the Secrets to Creating Lasting Value*. San Francisco: Jossey-Bass.

Ghosh, Koustab. 2015. "Developing Organizational Creativity and Innovation: Toward a Model of Self-Leadership, Employee Creativity, Creativity Climate and Workplace Innovative Orientation." *Management Research Review* 38, no. 11: 1126–48.

Ghosh, Koustab, and Naresh Khatri. 2017. "Does Servant Leadership Work in Hospitality Sector: A Representative Study in the Hotel Organizations." *Journal of Hospitality and Tourism Management*.

Gillespie, Nicole A., and Leon Mann. 2004. "Transformational Leadership and Shared Values: The Building Blocks of Trust." *Journal of Managerial Psychology* 19, no. 6: 588–607.

Goetz, Stephan J., and Sundar S. Shrestha. 2009. "Explaining Self-Employment Success and Failure: Wal-Mart versus Starbucks, or Schumpeter versus Putnam." *Social Science Quarterly* 90, no. 1: 22–38.

Goleman, Daniel. 1995. *Emotional Intelligence.* New York: Bantam Books.

Greenleaf, Robert K. 1977. *Servant Leadership: A Journey into the Nature of Legitimate Power and Greatness.* New York: Paulist Press.

Grosjean, Michael W., et al. 2004. "Leaders, Values, and Organizational Climate: Examining Leadership Strategies for Establishing an Organizational Climate Regarding Ethics." *Journal of Business Ethics* 55, no. 3: 223–41.

Gunn, Will A. 2016. "Military Leadership: Team Development through Mentoring and Coaching." *GP Solo* 33, no. 5: 26–9.

Hackman, M. Z., & Johnson, C. E. 2018. *Leadership: A Communication Perspective.* Long Grove, Illinois: Waveland Press, Inc.

Hambley, Laura A., Thomas A. O'Neill, and Theresa J. B. Kline. 2007. "Virtual Team Leadership: The Effects of Leadership Style and Communication Medium on Team Interaction Styles and Outcomes." *Organizational Behavior and Human Decision Processes* 103, no. 1: 1–20.

Hersey, Paul, Kenneth H. Blanchard, and Dewey E. Johnson. 2001. *Management of Organizational Behavior: Leading Human Resources.* Upper Saddle River, NJ: Prentice Hall.

Hietschold, Nadine, Ronny Reinhardt, and Sebastian Gurtner. 2020. "Who Put the 'NO' in Innovation? Innovation Resistance Leaders' Behaviors and Self-Identities." *Technological Forecasting and Social Change* 158: 120177.

Hitt, Michael A., and R. Duane Ireland. 2002. "The Essence of Strategic Leadership: Managing Human and Social Capital." *Journal of Leadership and Organizational Studies* 9, no. 1: 3–14.

Hudson, Valerie M., et al. 2008. "The Heart of the Matter: The Security of Women and the Security of States." *International Security* 33, no. 3: 7–45.

Hughes, David J., et al. 2018. "Leadership, Creativity, and Innovation: A Critical Review and Practical Recommendations." *The Leadership Quarterly* 29, no. 5: 549–69.

Hughes, Richard L., Katherine M. Beatty, and David Dinwoodie. 2013. *Becoming a Strategic Leader: Your Role in Your Organization's Enduring Success.* Somerset: John Wiley & Sons, Incorporated.

Hultman, Ken, and William Gellermann. 2002. *Balancing Individual and Organizational Values: Walking the Tightrope to Success.* San Francisco, CA: Jossey-Bass/Pfeiffer.

Hunt, James M., and Joseph R. Weintraub. 2007. *The Coaching Organization: A Strategy for Developing Leaders.* Thousand Oaks, CA: SAGE.

Ikeda, Kazuaki, and Anthony Marshall. 2016. "How Successful Organizations Drive Innovation." *Strategy & Leadership* 44, no. 3: 9–19.

Jaradat, Mohammad, and Sergiu-Dan Iurian. 2019. "Adapting Leadership Methods to Global Challenges: Interactive Leadership." *Calitatea* 20, no. 1: 487.

Jiang, Hua, Yi Luo, and Owen Kulemeka. 2016. "Leading in the Digital Age: A Study of How Social Media Are Transforming the Work of Communication Professionals." *Telematics and Informatics* 33, no. 2: 493–9.

Jiang, Zhenshuai. 2018. "A Comparative Study of the Concepts of Torah in the Hebrew Bible and Li in Zuozhuan." *Journal of Chinese Philosophy* 45, no. 3–4: 175–89.

Joachim, Verena, Patrick Spieth, and Sven Heidenreich. 2018. "Active Innovation Resistance: An Empirical Study on Functional and Psychological Barriers to Innovation Adoption in Different Contexts." *Industrial marketing management* 71: 95–107.

Johnson, Rebecca, Amy Grove, and Aileen Clarke. 2018. "It's Hard to Play Ball: A Qualitative Study of Knowledge Exchange and

Silo Effects in Public Health." *BMC Health Services Research* 18, no. 1: 1–11.

Karuvelil, George. 2015. "To Whom Am I Speaking?: Communication, Culture, and Fundamental Theology." *Theological Studies* 76, no. 4: 675–97.

Keenan, Jesse M. "COVID, Resilience, and the Built Environment." *Environment Systems & Decisions* 40.2 (2020): 216–21.

Keidel, Robert W. 1994. "Rethinking Organizational Design [and Executive Commentary]." *The Academy of Management Executive* 8, no. 4: 12–30.

Kernis, Michael H. 2003. "Toward a Conceptualization of Optimal Self-Esteem." *Psychological Inquiry* 14, no. 1: 1–26.

Khalili, Ashkan. 2016. "Linking Transformational Leadership, Creativity, Innovation, and Innovation-Supportive Climate." *Management decision* 54, no. 9: 2277–93.

Kipfer, Brent. 2017. "Thriving Under Persecution: Meserete Kristos Church Leadership During the Ethiopian Revolution (1974–1991)." *The Mennonite Quarterly Review* 91, no. 3: 297–369.

Kouzes, James M., and Barry Z. Posner. 2017. *The Leadership Challenge: How to Make Extraordinary Things Happen in Organizations*. New York: Wiley.

Krajcsák, Zoltán. 2018. "Making High Committed Workplaces by Strong Organizational Values." *Journal of Human Values* 24, no. 2: 127–37.

Kyvik, Oyvin. 2018. "The Global Mindset: A Must for International Innovation and Entrepreneurship." *International Entrepreneurship and Management Journal* 14, no. 2: 309–27.

Lan, Yuanyuan, Yuhuan Xia, and Lin Yang. 2021. "Effects of Servant Leadership on the Leader's Innovative Behavior." *Social Behavior and Personality* 49, no. 10: 1–13.

Lee, Yuk Ling Angie, et al. 2020. "Demystifying the Differences in the Impact of Training and Incentives on Employee Performance: Mediating Roles of Trust and Knowledge Sharing." *Journal of Knowledge Management* 24, no. 8: 1987–2006.

Levine, Michael P., and Jacqueline Boaks. 2014. "What Does Ethics Have to Do with Leadership?" *Journal of Business Ethics* 124, no. 2: 225–42.

Lewis, C. S. 1952. *Mere Christianity: A Revised and Enlarged Edition, with a New Introduction of the Three Books, the Case for Christianity, Christian Behaviour, and Beyond Personality*. New York: Macmillan.

Litchfield, Robert C., Cameron M. Ford, and Richard J. Gentry. 2015. "Linking Individual Creativity to Organizational Innovation." *The Journal of Creative Behavior* 49, no. 4: 279–94.

Mabey, Christopher, et al. 2017. "Having Burned the Straw Man of Christian Spiritual Leadership, What Can We Learn from Jesus about Leading Ethically?" *Journal of Business Ethics* 145, no. 4: 757–69.

Madestam, Jenny, and Lena Lid Falkman. 2017. "Rhetorical Construction of Political Leadership in Social Media." *Journal of Organizational Change Management* 30, no. 3: 299–311.

Marsh, Nick, Mike McAllum, and Dominique Purcell. 2002. *Strategic Foresight: The Power of Standing in the Future*. Melbourne: Crown Content.

Martin, S., ed. 2019. *Active Listening: Improve Your Ability to Listen and Lead*. Center for Creative Leadership Press.

Michalko, Michael. 2006. *Thinkertoys: A Handbook of Creative-Thinking Techniques*. Ten Speed Press.

Michelli, Joseph A. 2007. *The Starbucks Experience: 5 Principles for Turning Ordinary into Extraordinary*. New York: McGraw-Hill.

Miller, Kent D. 2017. "Organizing with the Spirit." *Christian Scholar's Review* 46, no. 3: 213.

Mizzell, Nathan, and Russell L. Huizing. 2018. "When Servant Leadership Fails: The Importance of Aligning Values." *Journal of Biblical Perspectives in Leadership* 8, no. 1: 12–24.

Momeny, Leonard Scott, and Michael Gourgues. 2019. "Communication that Develops: Clarity of Process on Transformational Leadership through Study of Effective Communication of Emotional Intelligence." *Christian Education Journal* 16, no. 2: 226–40.

Moore, Rickie D. 2007. "The Prophet as Mentor: A Crucial Facet of the Biblical Presentations of Moses, Elijah, and Isaiah." *Journal of Pentecostal Theology* 15, no. 2: 155–72.

Murari, Krishna, and Shankar Gupta Kripa. 2012. "Impact of Servant Leadership on Employee Empowerment." *Journal of Strategic Human Resource Management* 1, no. 1: 28.

Nadler, David A., and Michael L. Tushman. 1999. "The Organization of the Future: Strategic Imperatives and Core Competencies for the 21st Century." *Organizational Dynamics* 28, no. 1: 45–60.

Neill, Marlene S., and Hua Jiang. 2017. "Functional Silos, Integration & Encroachment in Internal Communication." *Public Relations Review* 43, no. 4: 850–62.

Northouse, Peter Guy. 2013. *Leadership: Theory and Practice.* Thousand Oaks: SAGE.

Oncken, William, III. 2000. "Ethics and Integrity." *Executive Excellence* 17, no. 5: 15.

Oster, G. 2009. "Christian Innovation: Descending into the Abyss of Light." *Regent Global Business Review* 3, no. 1: 17–22.

Oster, Gary. 2009. *Listening to Luddites: Innovation Antibodies and Corporate Success.* 10.

Padilla, Art, Robert Hogan, and Robert B. Kaiser. 2007. "The Toxic Triangle: Destructive Leaders, Susceptible Followers, and Conducive Environments." *The Leadership Quarterly* 18, no. 3: 176–94.

Parolini, Jeanine, Kathleen Patterson, and Bruce Winston. 2009. "Distinguishing between Transformational and Servant Leadership." *Leadership & Organization Development Journal* 30, no. 3: 274–91.

Passmore, Jonathan, et al. *Coaching Section I: The Wiley-Blackwell Handbook of the Psychology of Coaching and Mentoring.*

Patterson, Kathleen Ann. 2003. "Servant Leadership: A Theoretical Model." *ABI/INFORM Global.*

Paus, Viorica. 2013. "New Media and Leadership: Social Media and Open Organizational Communication." *Manager* 17: 73–8.

Pearson, Nathaniel. 2012. "The Servant-Mentor: Raising Up the Next Generation of Servant-Leaders." *The International Journal of Servant-Leadership* 8/9, no. 1: 345–60.

Peters, Richard, Joe M. Ricks, and Christopher Doval. 2017. "Jesus Centered Leadership and Business Applications: An Alternative Approach." *Business and Society Review* 122, no. 4: 589–612.

Pietraszewski, David. 2020. "The Evolution of Leadership: Leadership and Followership as a Solution to the Problem of Creating and Executing Successful Coordination and Cooperation Enterprises." *The Leadership Quarterly* 31, no. 2: 101299.

Pittenger, Khushwant K. S., and Beverly A. Heimann. 2000. "Building Effective Mentoring Relationships." *Review of Business* 21, no. 1: 38.

Posner, Barry Z. 2015. "An Investigation into the Leadership Practices of Volunteer Leaders." *Leadership & Organization Development Journal* 36, no. 7: 885–98.

Prentice, Mike, Marc Halusic, and Kennon M. Sheldon. 2014. "Integrating Theories of Psychological Needs-as-Requirements and Psychological Needs-as-Motives: A Two Process Model." *Social and Personality Psychology Compass* 8, no. 2: 73–85.

Raven, Bertram H., and John R. P. Frence Jr. 1958. *Journal of Personality* 26, no. 3: 400.

Reese, Simon. 2014. "Do Actions Speak Louder than Words—Study of a Shared Vision?" *Industrial and Commercial Training* 46, no. 5: 237–43.

Retzlaff, Kimberly J. 2020. "Staffing and Orientation during the COVID-19 Pandemic." *AORN Journal* 112, no. 3: 206–11.

Robbins, Vernon K. 1996. *Exploring the Texture of Texts: A Guide to Socio-Rhetorical Interpretation.* Valley Forge, PA: Trinity Press International.

Rodin, R. S. 2010. *The Steward Leader: Transforming People, Organizations, and Communities.* Westmont: InterVarsity Press.

Rothwell, William J. 2011. "Replacement Planning: A Starting Point for Succession Planning and Talent Management." *International Journal of Training and Development* 15, no. 1: 87–99.

Schein, Edgar H., and Peter Schein. 2016. *Organizational Culture and Leadership, 5ᵗʰ Edition*. John Wiley & Sons.

Schlagwein, Daniel, and Monica Hu. 2017. "How and Why Organisations Use Social Media: Five Use Types and their Relation to Absorptive Capacity." *Journal of Information Technology* 32, no. 2: 194–209.

———. 2018. "Correction to How and Why Organisations use Social Media: Five use Types and their Relation to Absorptive Capacity." *Journal of Information Technology* 33, no. 4: 361–2.

Schnabel, Eckhard J. 2008. *Paul the Missionary*. Illinois: InterVarsity Press.

Schüler, Julia, et al. 2019. "Implicit Motives and Basic Psychological Needs." *Journal of Personality* 87, no. 1: 37–55.

Schultz, Howard, and Dori Jones Yang. 1997. *Pour Your Heart into It: How Starbucks Built a Company One Cup at a Time*. New York, NY: Hyperion.

Schunemann, Julia. 2014. "Why Strategic Foresight Matters for Africa." *Institute for Security Studies Papers* 2014, no. 12: 12.

Schwartz, Mark S. 2016. "Ethical Decision-Making Theory: An Integrated Approach." *Journal of Business Ethics* 139, no. 4: 755–76.

Semedo, Ana Suzete Dias, Arnaldo Fernandes Matos Coelho, and Neuza Manuel Pereira Ribeiro. 2016. "Effects of Authentic Leadership, Affective Commitment and Job Resourcefulness on Employees' Creativity and Individual Performance." *Leadership & Organization Development Journal* 37, no. 8: 1038–55.

Sen Sendjaya, and James C. Sarros. 2002. "Servant Leadership: Its Origin, Development, and Application in Organizations." *Journal of Leadership & Organizational Studies* 9, no. 2: 57–64.

Sendjaya, Sen, James C. Sarros, and Joseph C. Santora. 2008. "Defining and Measuring Servant Leadership Behaviour in Organizations." *Journal of Management Studies* 45, no. 2: 402–24.

Shalley, Christina E., and Lucy L. Gilson. 2004. "What Leaders Need to Know: A Review of Social and Contextual Factors that Can Foster or Hinder Creativity." *The Leadership Quarterly* 15, no. 1: 33–53.

Shalley, Christina E., and Jill Perry-Smith. 2008. "The Emergence of Team Creative Cognition: The Role of Diverse Outside Ties, Sociocognitive Network Centrality, and Team Evolution." *Strategic Entrepreneurship Journal* 2, no. 1: 23–41.

Shamir, Boas, and Galit Eilam. 2005. "What's Your Story?" A Life-Stories Approach to Authentic Leadership Development." *The Leadership Quarterly* 16, no. 3: 395.

Sheldon, Kennon M. 2011. "Integrating Behavioral-Motive and Experiential-Requirement Perspectives on Psychological Needs: A Two Process Model." *Psychological Review* 118, no. 4: 552–69.

Sloan, David, Alan Mikkelson, and Timothy Wilkinson. 2020. "How to Communicate Servant-Leadership." *The International Journal of Servant-Leadership* 14, no. 1: 325–57.

Song, Jiying. 2018. "Leading through Awareness and Healing: A Servant-Leadership Model." *The International Journal of Servant-Leadership* 12, no. 1: 245–84.

Sosik, John J., and Dongil Jung. 2018. *Full Range Leadership Development: Pathways for People, Profit, and Planet*. Milton: Routledge.

Sousa, Milton, and Dirk Dierendonck. 2017. "Servant Leadership and the Effect of the Interaction between Humility, Action, and Hierarchical Power on Follower Engagement." *Journal of Business Ethics* 141, no. 1: 13–25.

Spears, L. C. 1998. *Insights on Leadership: Service, Stewardship, Spirit, and Servant-Leadership*. John Wiley & Sons, Inc.

———. 2002. "Tracing the Past, Present, and Future of Servant-Leadership." In *Focus on Leadership: Servant-Leadership for the 21ˢᵗ Century*, edited by L. C. Spears and M. Lawrence, 1–16. New York, NY: Wiley.

———. 2010. "Character and Servant Leadership: Ten Characteristics of Effective, Caring Leaders." *The Journal of Virtues & Leadership* 1, no. 1: 25–30.

Spielman, Larry. 1999. "David's Abuse of Power." *Word & World* 19, no. 3: 251–259.

Srivastava, Abhishek, Kathryn M. Bartol, and Edwin A. Locke. 2006. "Empowering Leadership in Management Teams: Effects on Knowledge Sharing, Efficacy, and Performance." *The Academy of Management Journal* 49, no. 6: 1239–51.

Starr, Julie. 2004. "The Manager's Role in Coaching." *Development and Learning in Organizations* 18, no. 2: 9–12.

Stavridis, James. 2017. "Challenges in Global Leadership." *The Fletcher Forum of World Affairs* 41, no. 2: 7–14.

Stenschke, Christoph W. 2017. "The Leadership Challenges of Paul's Collection for the Saints in Jerusalem: Part II: Overcoming the Obstacles on the Side of the Recipients and of Paul." *Verbum et Ecclesia* 38, no. 1.

Stoller, Eric. 2013. "Our Shared Future: Social Media, Leadership, Vulnerability, and Digital Identity." *Journal of College and Character* 14, no. 1: 5–10.

Sudiardhita, Ketut, et al. 2018. "The Effect of Compensation, Motivation of Employee and Work Satisfaction to Employee Performance." *Academy of Strategic Management Journal* 17, no. 4: 1–14.

Sun, Peter Y. T. 2013. *The Servant Identity: Influences on the Cognition and Behavior of Servant Leaders.* 24.

Srivastava, A., K. M. Bartol, and E. A. Locke. 2006. "Empowering Leadership in Management Teams: Effects on Knowledge Sharing, Efficacy, and Performance." *The Academy of Management Journal* 49, no. 6: 1239–1251.

Talpau, A., and D. Boscor. 2011. "Customer-Oriented Marketing—a Strategy that Guarantees Success: Starbucks and McDonald's." *Bulletin of the Transilvania University of Brașov* 4, no. 1: 51–8.

Thompson, Amy, Cleve Sylvester, and John Ahern. 2019. "Treating Others with Respect Is a Core Value." *Army* 69, no. 9: 7–9.

Tzu, S., D. Galvin, L. Giles, and G. Stade. 2003. *The Art of War.* New York: Barnes & Noble Classics.

Uhl-Bien, Mary. 2021. "Complexity and COVID-19: Leadership and Followership in a Complex World." *Journal of Management Studies* 58, no. 5: 1400–4.

US Army. n.d. "The Army's Vision and Strategy." https://www.army. mil/about/.

Valk, John. 2010. "Leadership for Transformation: The Impact of a Christian Worldview." *Journal of Leadership Studies* 4, no. 3: 83–6.

Van Dierendonck, Dirk, and Inge Nuijten. 2011. "The Servant Leadership Survey: Development and Validation of a Multidimensional Measure." *Journal of Business and Psychology* 26, no. 3: 249–67.

Van Dierendonck, Dirk, and Kathleen Patterson. 2015. "Compassionate Love as a Cornerstone of Servant Leadership: An Integration of Previous Theorizing and Research." *Journal of Business Ethics* 128, no. 1: 119–31.

Van Eck, Ernest. 2014. "The Harvest and the Kingdom: An Interpretation of the Sower (Mk 4:3b–8) as a Parable of Jesus the Galilean." *Hervormde Teologiese Studies* 70, no. 1: 1–10.

VanOtten, George A. 2005. "Culture Matters." *Military Intelligence Professional Bulletin* 31, no. 1: 30–7.

Viljoen, Francois P. 2019. "Why Jesus Spoke in Parables." *In die Skriflig / In Luce Verbi* 53, no. 1.

Vince, Russ. 2014. "What Do HRD Scholars and Practitioners Need to Know about Power, Emotion, and HRD?" *Human Resource Development Quarterly* 25, no. 4: 409–20.

Weiss, Matthias, Markus Baer, and Martin Hoegl. 2022. "The Human Side of Innovation Management: Bridging the Divide between the Fields of Innovation Management and Organizational Behavior." *The Journal of Product Innovation Management* 39, no. 3: 283–91.

Whittington, J. Lee, et al. 2005. "Legacy Leadership: The Leadership Wisdom of the Apostle Paul." *The Leadership Quarterly* 16, no. 5: 749–70.

Will, George. 2000. "Moral Leadership." *Leadership Excellence* 17, no. 5: 15.

Williams, Wallace Alexander Jr, et al. 2017. "Servant Leadership and Followership Creativity: The Influence of Workplace Spirituality and Political Skill." *Leadership & Organization Development Journal* 38, no. 2: 178–93.

Winston, Bruce E. and Patterson, Kathleen. 2006. *An Integrative Definition of Leadership*. 1.

Witzel, Eddy. 2014. "Mentor." *The Journal of Applied Christian Leadership* 8, no. 1: 90.

Yeung, Edward, and Winny Shen. 2019. "Can Pride Be a Vice and Virtue at Work? Associations between Authentic and Hubristic Pride and Leadership Behaviors." *Journal of Organizational Behavior* 40, no. 6: 605–24.

Youssef, Carolyn M., and Fred Luthans. 2012. "Positive Global Leadership." *Journal of World Business* 47, no. 4: 539–47.

Zaprometova, Olga M. 2018. "From Persecution to 'Prosperity.'" *Journal of the European Pentecostal Theological Association* 38, no. 2: 138–49.

Zeni, Thomas A., et al. 2016. "Making 'Sense' of Ethical Decision Making." *The Leadership Quarterly* 27, no. 6: 838–55.

Zhou, A., Y. Liu, X. Su, and H. Xu. 2019. "Gossip Fiercer than a Tiger: Effect of Workplace Negative Gossip on Targeted Employees' Innovative Behavior." *Social Behavior and Personality: An International Journal* 47, no. 5: 1–11.

Zhou, Jing, and Jennifer M. George. 2003. "Awakening Employee Creativity: The Role of Leader Emotional Intelligence." *The Leadership Quarterly* 14, no. 4: 545–68.

Ziek, Paul, and Stacy Smulowitz. 2014. "The Impact of Emergent Virtual Leadership Competencies on Team Effectiveness." *Leadership & Organization Development Journal* 35, no. 2: 106–20.

ABOUT THE AUTHOR

Bobbi is the director of Veterans Affairs for Washington County, Pennsylvania. She is a retired army veteran with a heart for veterans and a passion for leadership. While on active duty, she earned a bachelor's degree in information technology, a master's degree in organizational management, and her doctorate in strategic leadership at Regent University.

Bobbi's mission is to honor veterans and provide teaching and insight into leadership through articles, books, and speaking engagements.

Bobbi and her husband, Nevin, live in Southwest Pennsylvania and have been married for thirty years. They have two children and one grandson.